D0765181

Same Sex, Different Cultures

Same Sex, Different Cultures

Gays and Lesbians Across Cultures

Gilbert Herdt

WestviewPress

A Division of HarperCollins*Publishers*

Chapter 3 reprints approximately five pages of Gilbert Herdt, "Fetish and Fantasy in Sambia Initiation," which was originally published as chapter 3 of Gilbert Herdt, ed., *Rituals of Manhood: Male Initiation in Papua New Guinea* (Berkeley: University of California Press, 1982).

Published in 1997 in the United States of America by Westview Press, 5500 Central Avenue, Boulder, Colorado 80301-2877, and in the United Kingdom by Westview Press, 12 Hid's Copse Road, Cumnor Hill, Oxford OX2 9JJ

Library of Congress Cataloging-in-Publication Data
Herdt, Gilbert H., 1949–
  Same sex, different cultures : gays and lesbians across cultures /
Gilbert Herdt.
    p. cm.
  Includes bibliographical references and index.
  ISBN 0-8133-3163-3
  1. Homosexuality. 2. Lesbianism. 3. Gay men—Cross-cultural
studies. 4. Lesbians—Cross-cultural studies. I. Title.
GN484.35.H47 1997
306.76'6—dc21   97-1839
                                                                                              CIP

The paper used in this publication meets the requirements of the American National Standard for Permanence of Paper for Printed Library Materials Z39.48-1984.

10   9   8   7   6   5   4   3   2   1

To the memory of Ruth Benedict

◀ Contents ▶

◀ **Preface** ▶

TO DESIRE THE SAME GENDER and to create relationships based on love and sex with another man or woman are to stake a claim on history and culture. This is true not only because those who have openly dared to love the same gender have been punished and forced to flee from their own lands. It is also true because controversies surrounding homosexuality remain a vital part of the debate about what is "normal and natural" in the range of sexual variation and the tolerance accorded sexual minorities in all human societies. Fortunately, we live in a time in which the story of gays and lesbians across cultures and in the United States is being uncovered and in this way liberated from political censorship and repression. The history of persons who have desired the same gender is also being rewritten in order to understand and reclaim the "lost" and "invisible" lives of gays and lesbians hidden from society and hidden from history. This is the spirit in which I have written this book: to open the world of sexual lifeways across cultures to readers who would like to understand the place of their own sexuality and their own sexual culture in that world.

Let me begin the introduction to this book with my own journey to New Guinea. It was early September 1974 when I set off by foot from the Marawaka Patrol Station in the Eastern Highlands Province of the New Guinea Highlands, where I first met the Sambia people. In those days there were no roads or airstrips. I trekked two and a half days across three mountain chains to their isolated valleys and villages. As I traveled from place to place in search of a field site, I was struck by the lonely beauty of the jungles and the steady and confident way in which these peoples had preserved a valued way of life in the face of constant warfare and the difficulties of the climate and land. On entering the village, I was taken directly to the men's house, for there the elders and war leaders held council, and they would decide my fate. Out in the plaza of the hamlet were a swarm of happy faces of children, the younger ones shy, the older ones openly curious about the strange white man who had come from the outside. But inside the men's house I was surrounded by a group of strong young warriors and much younger ritual initiates who made up the core of the village fighting force in times of war. They were the pride and hope of the village, the next generation that would assume the mantle of power and the hard work of hunting and building gardens that made the Sambia economy. How could I guess that these men and boys were all active participants in an ancient ritual complex of homoerotic relations that in all likelihood stretched thousands of years into the dim past? Even less could I imagine that such a structure of same-gender relations was the very means by which masculinity was created not only in Sambia culture but also in all the neighboring societies that have now been studied.

It was impossible for me to understand this at the time, even though I was myself very sensitive to exploring how to express my emerging same-gender desires. I had grown up in a society in which everyone assumed that I was heterosexual, including my parents, and so did I. As a child in a small town in rural Kansas in the 1950s, homosexuality was barely whispered about as a sin and disease of terrible proportions. In fact, I never heard the word *homosexual* or *faggot* spoken until I got into high school, and there I sensed that it was an accusation to be avoided, if at all possible, because of the permanent stigma and dishonor it brought. Like most of the people of my generation, it was only in college, away from family and community, that I began to experiment with sexuality as an adult, first thinking of myself as "bisexual" in my relations with women and other men. In the late 1960s I attended university in California, and there, for the first time, I experienced intimacy with a male friend in college. But those days were so filled with study and work, amid protests against the Vietnam War and the now-long-vanished cultural happenings of the "peace and freedom" movement and "hippies," that my sexual experimentation seemed characteristic of the time. Only as the gay and lesbian movement took hold and I began to think of myself as "gay" did I start to practice a new identity and role—and this carried more significant consequences for my standing in society and in the academic hierarchy. After all, homophobia and violence against gays and lesbians were accepted. It was about this time, however, that I headed off to New Guinea—a period that was to forever change my life.

I am a cultural anthropologist, classically trained in the old-fashioned mode, which requires many years of fieldwork in many different "field trips" to understand how life is lived in another culture. To be welcomed into a small village community and be adopted as one of its own; to learn an unwritten language and immerse oneself in the strange customs and foods of a place far removed from one's own people and place; to feel the emotions and the troubles of these people as they encounter the eternal rhythm of birth and marriage and death; and to befriend and understand how the people themselves reflect on what it means to be a Sambia from birth until the grave—these are the basic and enriching as well as the most humbling experiences a human being can ever know. In the field of anthropology as well as in the other social sciences that deal with such problems, many of these issues have been written about at length. Nearly always, however, sexuality is left out or sometimes wiped clean from the pages of the book that emerges from study. But if this is true for sexuality in general, and much of what counts as heterosexuality, how much more true it is for homosexuality and bisexuality and the understanding of lesbians and gays in particular! And here is where my experience was special among the Sambia.

After living in the men's house for some weeks before a house of my own could be built in the center of the village, I had befriended several of the young men of my own age and become comfortable and close with the ten- and twelve-year-old boys who lived in the clubhouse. Although I knew from travelers' reports that the males in this general area supposedly engaged in same-sex relations, I had not seen anything of the kind during the first months of my fieldwork in 1974. Moreover, I had specifically asked the dumb question "Do you have sex with other boys?" which typically brought dumb answers or laughs. The men routinely denied homosexuality, much as has been reported for New Guinea for decades and as is still routinely reported, as we see in Chapter 3, for the whole continent of

Africa. It is no wonder that heterosexual anthropologists, faced with the absence of any observable sexual relations and the denial of homosexuality, have concluded that homosexuality was "absent" or "rare" or "abnormal," as the case may be (Benedict 1934; Herdt 1981, 1984a).

But as Margaret Mead (1961) once warned long ago, and my teacher Kenneth Read (1980) reiterated, we must be cautious about reports that state the absence of a trait in the absence of direct observation or close investigation. However, I accepted the men's reports, and became skeptical of western observers who naively concluded that when people of the same gender held hands, they must therefore be sexually intimate. That was their ethnocentrism, I felt. The men and the boys in the clubhouse were intensely intimate and lived in extraordinarily close circumstances, for the houses were small and without compartments. But I saw no sexual activity.

What I did know was that a whole secret world of ritual initiation established a firm and powerful barrier between the men and the women and children, who were officially excluded from the ceremonies and from the men's house in general. Beginning in 1975, I was permitted to observe a series of sixteen different ritual initiations, from the first-stage initiation ceremonies, performed on an age-set of boys aged seven to ten, to the final, sixth-stage initiations, performed for young adult men in their twenties, on the occasion of the birth of their first child. During these months I saw for the first time that the boys were initiated into the men's house through sacred body rituals that required them to be "cleansed" of pollution from their mothers, followed by insemination by the older boys in order for them to grow big and strong. During the period of these initiations there were long periods of waiting and preparation, and I set out to learn the language and develop rapport with several Sambia males, my key informants. I have written about each of them in depth elsewhere (Herdt 1987b; Herdt and Stoller 1990). These Sambia men included Kanteilo, an elder (aged sixty) and the man who sponsored me in the village; Tali, a middle-aged man who was a ritual expert; Wieyu, a younger man of my own age (twenty-five), recently married and a father; and Moondi, a youth in the process of making the transition from being an "initiate" (semen recipient) to a young bachelor (adolescent semen donor), following his third-stage "puberty" ceremony around the age of fifteen. They were my closest male friends and collaborators and the source of my deepest insight into Sambia culture and secret ritual. My closest female Sambia friends, especially Penjuwki (in her midtwenties), were the source of detailed knowledge about the women's world as well, but with them I could never discuss male homoerotic relationships since these were secret. But all of my male friends grew up believing that same-sex relations were the most "natural and normal" part of human development—and absolutely vital to the growth and ritual purity of the male body and mind.

By living with the Sambia for the first two years, in 1974–1976, and returning for field trips in 1979, 1981, 1983, 1985, 1987, 1989, 1990, and, last, 1993, I came to develop a more reflective sense of my own homoerotic feelings as well. These feelings no longer seemed strange or unnatural, or the antithesis of masculinity, as my own society had interpreted these things. I came gradually to accept as a normal part of my self-concept and body sensibility desires and intimate feelings for other males. Of course, during these years not only was I maturing and aging, but also the United States was changing in the direction of increasing tolerance toward homosexuality. The lesbian and gay movement and the bisexual movement have since made many advances that have generally opened up sexuality and gender relations in more positive ways for everyone in American society. This has not been without its costs and pain to society, and there are many limitations and strings attached to the tolerance of homosexuality, for sexual discrimination and violence continue to be a threat against the normal social life of all lesbians and gay men.

But these problems are far removed from Sambia culture. In Sambia society, by contrast, to be "normal and natural" is to be inseminated by another man and then to take the role of inseminator, first to a boy, and then to a woman, at a later stage following marriage. The Sambia believe that for a man and a woman to attain full adult personhood, they must be married and produce children. Only then, they reckon, can the clan and society continue. In short, the Sambia do not have a concept of homosexuality in the western sense of the term. This may seem strange coming from a society in which same-gender relations among males are universal during the years from age seven to age twenty or so. But that is because, for the Sambia, sexuality is a ritual process, involving the body as a kind of temple and template of society, in which sex can never be isolated or separated from the larger social context of family, kinship, religion, and community. This cultural worldview about sexual lifeways is indeed common to many nonwestern peoples, even if same-sex relations are not.

Living among the Sambia and understanding their culture thus came to shape and influence my own sexuality and the sense in which I defined and accepted myself as being gay and in a partnership for life with another man in my own society. Just as one might expect, it was very important to my Sambia friends not only that I was interested in their customs and could be trusted to keep the secrets of the initiation rituals from the women and children, but also that I was curious and comfortable about their homoerotic relations. I understood their feelings well enough. And I was sensitive enough to inquire about issues of sexual attraction and excitement that another person in my position might have found offensive or repulsive if he lacked the experience or curiosity to go on.

But equally true, as the years went by, the Sambia could not understand my own sexuality, and even my closest friends, such as Weiyu and Moondi, would implore me to consider getting married and having children. They even tried to arrange a marriage for me with a Sambia woman, and on more than one occasion, because they felt "sorry" for me! More than once I can remember Moondi asking about my relationship with my "friend" (partner) in the United States; and I even used the world *gay* to refer to this relationship, but Moondi was unable to understand what this meant to me. I had reached the limits of cross-cultural understanding even among the people closest to me in Sambia culture. Their society did not have a concept for homosexual or gay, and these notions, when I translated them in the appropriate way, were alien and unmanageable.

Thus, it is remarkable for me to think that, even though living with the Sambia enabled me to accept in a way perhaps strange to the United States a concept of same-sex relations as normal and natural, the Sambia in their own way could only regard my own culture's identity constructs of homosexual and gay as strange. Herein lies a powerful lesson about the cross-cultural study of homosexuality—and a warning about the importance of being careful in the statements and assumptions we make about another people, as well as the need to respect their own customs for what they are—and are not.

What is the "purpose" of a lesbian or gay life? Is it possible to find a productive and meaningful place in society, to have a career, to fall in love, to make a definite contribution that will last? Such unlikely questions were first raised in my own mind not when I was growing up in rural Kansas but only later when I found myself in the role of teaching about these things in Chicago and Amsterdam.

The gay or lesbian person—whether a student completing high school and entering college, a person who is beginning a career, or a person who is entering midlife, as is much of the baby-boom generation that now contemplates its "legacy" in society—is more than at any other time in history a citizen of the global culture of lesbians and gays. Today we are seeing the controversies of our societies—such as the question of gays serving with honor in the military, the right to the social entitlements and respect of being a member of a sexual minority, the rights of lesbians to mother children and rear them with their partners, the rights of lesbians and gay men to marry and adopt children—being reviewed and debated as never before. The images of gay life in the past are being painted in the light of new histories of lesbians and gays. They speak to utopian visions of the future as much as they did a hundred years ago, but with a better promise of fulfillment.

And the same holds true for the study of culture: To know of the existence of people who have loved and been intimate sexually and romantically with the same gender in other lands through divergent cultural practices and social roles is to know better what it means to be human. To reflect critically on what society teaches about homosexuality by looking at it in light of the knowledge of other cultures must be one of the general aims of anthropology. This led me in turn from doing fieldwork in New Guinea to initiating a new study of lesbian and gay youths in Chicago in 1987. There I was to find the fundamental question "What is the purpose of a gay life?" again posed to me, but this time by an eighteen-year-old boy, one of the teenagers whom we interviewed in our University of Chicago study of gay and lesbian development. His questions prompted me to write about the subject in a way different from before, looking at the general process of the formation of gay culture in the United States (Herdt 1992) as well as the effects of AIDS on these culture processes (Herdt and Lindenbaum 1992). Here I initiated an anthropological study of gay and lesbian culture and development to understand the coming out process and sexual identity development in gay and lesbian self-identified youths in Chicago in the late 1980s. This work resulted in three major works: *Gay and Lesbian Youth* (1989); *Gay Culture in America: Essays from the Field* (1992); and, most recently, *Children of Horizons: How Gay and Lesbian Youth Are Forging a New Way Out of the Closet* (1996, coauthored with Andrew Boxer). In these latter three studies I have suggested that a fundamental break with history has occurred in the past "closet" generation, splitting apart the older cultural form of the closet homosexual from the newer form of the gay or lesbian who is out.

Through an examination of certain historical structures of sexual dimorphism, I have come to conclude that the identity categories "homosexual/heterosexual" in the nineteenth century and "gay/straight" in the twentieth century should be understood not as universal but as suggestions of common themes around the world (Herdt ed. 1994). In the study on the emergence of gay and lesbian youths in Chicago (Herdt and Boxer 1996), I have suggested that the nineteenth-century closet homosexual is a dying form of selfhood, but one that remains in competition with the newer gay or lesbian selfhood. It is precisely the intense form of the argument about what is universal and what is particular in sexual and gender structures that has led to the insights contained in this book. The rituals of "coming out," I have previously argued, have paved the way for new conditions of selfhood: a new kind of social contract with the self and gay community (Herdt ed. 1992). But what kind of a social and intimate self inhabits this form and occupies its bodies?

The question arose again in the context of my teaching courses at the University of Amsterdam, in the Netherlands, beginning in 1991 and through a sabbatical in 1992–1993. This experience and the joy of claiming Holland as my second home have come to strongly influence my sense of the cross-cultural issues. My students in Amsterdam and Nijmegan Universities, who were, of course, Dutch, made it clear that the question had never occurred to them in any simple sense, for homosexuality was much more accepted in their society. And yet when I listened to what they had to say about the cultural issues of gay roles and institutions and the problems of coming out in diverse settings, I recognized that this question underlay much of their thought. Likewise, as I evolved a course on the anthropology of sexual cultures for my students at the University of Chicago over the years, I began to think further about how gays and lesbians might live in other cultures.

Many of the scholars who are doing basic research on homosexuality in all of the arts and sciences are themselves lesbians or gay men who have sought to "set the record straight." Anthropology is no different. Within the field of anthropology, it seems, there has been no special protection from societal homophobia and scientific disinterest. Heterosexual fieldworkers have often been uninterested in or unwilling to sufficiently describe the lives of gays and lesbians in other cultures (Kulick and Willson 1995). Here is where an important general principle of culture and language study applies: The fieldworker must want to understand the Other sufficiently to overcome her or his own biases or the cultural blinders of her or his own background (Herdt and Stoller 1990). Anthropologists have in some cases been unable to enter the thought worlds of homoerotic roles and relationships in other cultures because they lacked the curiosity, empathy, or understanding to learn about homosexuality. For this reason, gay- and lesbian-identified anthropologists are making new headway in a fascinating and fast-changing sexual landscape of field study (Lewin and Leap 1996).

A decade ago it would not have been possible to write an introductory work on the anthropology of gay men and lesbians or to write their history and compare their cultures for the purpose of understanding the meanings of their same-sex desires and relationships. A taboo on the study of homosexuality surrounded the subject when I was myself an undergraduate and then a graduate student in the late 1960s and through the mid-1970s. The scientific study of sexuality was nascent, and the prohibition on the study of homosexuality in the social sciences, including anthropology, created terrible, seemingly impregnable barriers. Students in anthropology, sociology, history, literature, and allied fields found it nearly impossible to study same-sex desires, homosexuality, and gender roles, especially in other cultures. Happily, this taboo is breaking down. Thanks to the dedication of a few rare scholars from earlier generations of anthropology, beginning with Ruth Benedict and later followed by Kenneth Read, a whole generation of outstanding field anthropologists of my own generation emerged to provide a new standard of research, including Esther Newton, Joseph Carrier, Carole Vance, Steven Murray, Ralph Bolton, Richard Parker, Ellen Lewin, and Walter Williams, among others too numerous to mention (but see Weston 1993). Their work provides a beacon for enlightened people everywhere who seek a more far-reaching understanding of the meanings of sexuality, gender, and lives—to do justice to the immense diversity of sexual lifeways.

This book is meant as introduction only. Because of its general nature, I have been unable to cover many cultural cases, and the ones I do consider must be abbreviated and many historical and cultural details left out. For a broader and deeper understanding of historical cases, I recommend David Greenberg's (1988) monumental study *The Construction of Homosexuality* as the best all-around general study. For the United States, I recommend the recent study by Stephen Murray (1996), *American Gay*; the historical work of Esther Newton (1993), *Cherry Grove, Fire Island—Sixty Years in America's First Gay and Lesbian Town*; and George Chauncey Jr.'s *Gay New York* (1994). On the issues of sexual dimorphism, I recommend my own edited volume *Third Sex, Third Gender: Sexual Dimorphism in Culture and History* (1994). The specialist knows that these works—the product of decades of scholarship—only begin to capture the explosion of the wider literature. But for the beginning student, they constitute a small but wonderful body of theory, constructs, and accounts with which to begin examining same-gender lifeways around the world.

I owe a special thanks to Martin Duberman, who first encouraged me to write this book. I am also very indebted to my partner, Niels Teunis, for his guidance and assistance in dealing with the cultural study of same-gender relations in Africa and Holland. For helpful comments, I also thank Andy Boxer, Theo van der Meer, Paul Abramson, Bill Leap, and Heather Lindquist.

Finally, I dedicate this book to Ruth Benedict, poet, anthropologist, and humanist. Her love of women and of humanity in general in the earlier part of this century as well as her bravery in expressing a positive tolerance for homosexuality in her publications makes of her a woman for all ages. Such an inspiring legacy brings honor not only to anthropology and other fields that aspire to define something of the truth in other cultures, but also to all scholars who call themselves lesbian or gay.

Gilbert Herdt

◀ 1 ▶

Introduction: Gays and Lesbians Across Cultures

BEING DIFFERENT OR STANDING OUT from the crowd has never been easy, whether in New Guinea, Holland, the United States, or anywhere else. In all societies there are laws and rules to obey, and their violation may be punished—even by death—when the majority feels that the social order is sufficiently threatened. Sexuality is always a part of this order, and it is subject to many social controls, being close to marriage and reproduction and often regarded by religion as a sacred core of morality. Incest, for example, is nearly everywhere a prohibition against sex between certain close relatives. We are not surprised by this taboo and indeed so often take for granted cultural restrictions on behavior that these become a given part of our own folk view of "human nature." We learn to accommodate ourselves to these laws and rules as if they were perfectly normal and natural, when in fact such notions are regarded as foreign in neighboring communities.

For these reasons sexuality is often closely tied to societal definitions of a "man" or a "woman," to rules of social order and hierarchy, and to beliefs about what is "natural and normal." In each of these areas those who threaten or disrupt the social order are typically regarded as subversive in the usual sense of political revolutionaries or religious heretics whose actions or existence challenges the status quo. It is no wonder that sexual reform and liberation movements in many lands are thought to be the work of a nation's ene-

1

mies. But most people living within the folds of a tradition do not think of themselves in such terms, for they are neither revolutionaries nor heretics, often asking little more than to earn a living, to have friends and family, and to live out the expectations of the surrounding culture.

But what happens when ordinary citizens have divergent or forbidden desires for romance and sexual intimacy with others of their own gender? Here we find a fundamental dilemma—that their very existence as sexual and gendered persons goes directly against the grain of the culture. For millions of people around the world, this crisis of sexual being—of having bodies and desires at odds with the heteronormal roles and folk theory of human nature in their society—is not simply a theory. It produces turmoil and fear in their daily lives and the insistent need to conform and pretend or hide their sexual being. Indeed, it is this individual-against-society dilemma that dominates the history of homosexuality in the western tradition and is common to the problems of understanding gays and lesbians across cultures. The name of this fear is "homophobia." For the past three hundred years, its hostile attitude has confronted all boys and girls, men and women, who have loved the same gender—and dared to risk the sanctions of society in expressing the crisis of their sexual desires. That is the story of this book.

A great American anthropologist, Ruth Benedict, herself a woman who loved women, was fond of telling a creation story that comes from the Digger Indians of California and offers an insight into the cultural plight of lesbians and gays. According to the Indians, "In the beginning God gave to every people a cup, a cup of clay, and from this cup they drank their life." (The metaphor depicts how each culture is made distinctive and unique to its people.) In the old days, Benedict's informant said, the Indians had far more power than now. "Our cup is broken now. It has passed away" (Benedict 1934, 22). Benedict offered the myth as an affirmation of the broad spectrum of cultural lifeways that anthropologists have found and witnessed in passing from around the world. The myth speaks to a broader ideal of cultural diversity that is essential to belief in the western liberal democracy traditions in which anthropology is itself grounded.

In another way, however, the Digger Indians' myth also conveys the loss of tradition or custom—and the devastation that occurs when a culture is broken and its people are scattered. "Our cup is broken": The metaphor imagines a world in which the grace and beauty, the history and identity, of a people are lost and they are deprived of cherished stories of a lifeway. Since it is culture that provides much of the richness and meaning in human life, to be deprived of the support of one's cultural heritage is tantamount to social death and banishment from all that is worth holding in life. Such a poignant image of the broken cup speaks today to the historical and political suppression of homosexuality in many lands, as much as to the strong idealism and utopian strivings of gays and lesbians who have formed social movements for positive change over the past century. The image also symbolizes a kind of fabled diaspora and a present search for a home—a positive and loving culture—that will accept and cherish lesbians and gays as people who desire and love the same gender as a part of their perceived human nature.

Cultural Concepts of Homosexuality

Anthropology has shown that people who erotically desire the same gender sufficiently to organize their social lives around this desire come in all genders, colors, political and religious creeds, and nationalities. There is no special kind of person who is homosexual; and much as we might expect, there is no single word or construct, including the western idea of "homosexuality," that represents them all. To make matters even more complicated, the local term in each culture or community that classifies the homoerotic act or role is not always positive; indeed, in the western tradition it is usually negative. And people typically shun what is negative. We should be aware, however, that, even though there is no uniform term for the desire to love and have sexual intimacy with others of the same gender, and even though it may be negative or stigmatizing to be placed in such a category, many persons have dared to brave the consequences: economic loss and social stigma, censure and ostracism, even punishment, imprisonment, or death in the harshest disapproving cultures, such as the Soviet Union and the United States as they were in the Cold War.

Sexual practices "without sexuality" are one of the greatest problems faced by the anthropologist in studying same-gender relations across cultures. How does the anthropologist describe the lifeways of people who engage in homoerotic relations in the absence of the very idea of homosexuality? This is a constant source of intellectual trouble for the outsider who would study a local culture that lacks an equivalent to the western concept. Typically, the western observer assumes that someone who has sex with others of his or her gender is identified as a "homosexual." But the sky is not always blue; it is more often gray. In a variety of cultures around the world, and even within many communities within the United States, certain individuals of both genders and of distinct ethnic groups engage in homoerotic encounters, but they do not identify themselves as "homosexual" or "gay" or "lesbian" or even "bisexual." Quite the contrary, they may even be appalled by the idea of homosexuality when it is explained to them, and they cannot think of what being "that way" would feel like even when it is pointed out that they typically have sexual relations with the same gender. They may regard themselves as "heterosexuals," "straights," or just "human beings" who on occasion participate in homoerotic encounters for various reasons, including pleasure, money, social expectations, and the absence of other sexual opportunities. It is too easy to say that they have a "false consciousness," for their understanding is widely shared and even supported by the culture. That they may be afraid or oppressed and unable to self-identify as homosexual or gay are important factors to consider. Given the history of sexual repression in western countries, it is certainly reasonable to remember the stories of people who were "hidden in history" and could not "come out" until recent times (Duberman et al. 1989).

Likewise, in the United States today the cultural classification of sexual and gendered distinctions has created a huge diversity of positive and negative labels. These include "heterosexual," "homosexual," "bisexual," "queer," "straight," "gay," "lesbian," "dyke," "faggot," and "queen." Notice how often these labels come in pairs: heterosexual/homosexual, gay/straight, and so on. Western culture, it seems, has a penchant for dualisms and binary oppositions, in sexuality and gender as much as in other areas of nature and culture classification (Lévi-Strauss 1964). Although this is just a partial listing, it is striking to see that American culture has produced such a range of homoerotic labels, which also contribute to the valuations and attitudes surrounding sexual identities. We cannot hope to fully understand the meanings of these identities unless we investigate their basis in history and cultural lifeways. This is the reason that cultural relativism—the valuing of a culture in and of itself and not through its moralistic comparison with any other—is of overriding importance in teaching respect for the differences suggested by the beliefs and practices of other cultures as well as of sexual minorities in the western tradition.

The many terms that might be employed to refer to same-gender relations, including the terms *bisexual, gay,* and *lesbian* in western cultures, must be understood as situated historical passageways, as spaces in a larger house of uncertain construction and indefinite number of rooms, none of which should be a priori privileged over others. This is why I generally avoid using the term *homosexuality*—not to be "politically correct" but to be more accurate by employing the neutral descriptor *same-gender sexual relations.* This term means that people engage in sex with others who have the same genitals as themselves. (In fact, what really matters is what sociologist Harold Garfinkle once called the "cultural genitals," as these are valued as icons in society; but we get to that in later chapters.) People in many cultures are unwilling to identify themselves with a category term or construct such as homosexuality, and we should respect their right to do so. They may be quiet or shy about expressing what they most desire, particularly when it goes against the grain; and there is good reason to be reticent in openly expressing same-gender desires in repressive societies. More often, in cultures that disapprove of homosexuality, people try to accommodate and blend in, to find what satisfaction they can through compromised relationships of marriage and friendship and extramarital same-gender relations.

In this regard we must remember that in virtually all cultures around the world full personhood is not achievable until people have married and produced children. Otherwise, they go about the business of life trying their best to avoid conflict over these matters, for, after all, even though sexuality is extremely important in human life, there are many other equally important aspects of existence. Or people may come in time to regard themselves as "strange" or "different" or "eccentric" because they enjoy intimacy with others of their own gender. The difference may have to do in large measure with whether they actually carry their desires for love and intimacy over into sexual relations. One of the lessons of the cross-cultural record is that when they do, cultures vary immensely in their response.

The words that we choose in describing these homoerotic feelings and relationships are thus of real importance, both for what they include and what they exclude. In the western historical tradition, as classical scholars have shown, no Greek or Latin word corresponds to the modern concept of homosexuality, and this should give us pause in understanding the matrix of words that surround homosexuality. Although sexual relations among the Greeks occurred between persons of the same gender, and these are widely attested by the ancient sources, there is no notion that they were systematically classified or differentiated from others, nor were they made into a uniform category (Halperin 1990). And even though modern sexuality in western cultures is generally preoccupied with the gender of the sexual partners, in many parts of the world, including ancient Greece and Rome, it was the sexual act that mattered, which was reckoned in terms of the categories "penetrator" and "penetrated." A man could honorably engage in sexual relations with a woman or with a boy so long as he remained in the socially dominant or senior position of being the penetrator for phallic pleasure. Way into the early modern period desires for both genders were not regarded as very strange for most people (Trumbach 1994). We cannot therefore speak in such general terms of homosexuality in the ancient world or up until the nineteenth century. Neither, in most cases, can we speak of unitary categories of people, such as "the homosexual," "the heterosexual," or "the gay/lesbian," in many societies and historical cultures of the nonwestern world, right up to the present century, for the same reasons.

History reports that people who desired the same gender referred to themselves by a variety of local concepts—molly, queer, fairy, or, in the last century, homosexual, invert—in western countries such as England and the United States (Chauncey 1994; Greenberg 1988; Murray 1996; Trumbach 1994). Outside of the cities, however, and even in neighborhoods of the same urban center, such cultural terms often had secret or privileged meanings that were apparently unknown to large numbers of people—even those who might have aspired to express their same-gender desires through experimentation with these concepts had they known about them. Only in the twentieth century, through mass media and political rhetoric, has the explicit terminology of "homosexuality/heterosexuality" been widely applied to people and acts and events, typically to contain and control all sexual behavior. Only as wide-scale sexual liberation movements gained steam in the 1960s did people who desired the same gender begin to call themselves "lesbian" or "gay." Since that time these identity systems have been exported to other cultures, which has created controversies in developing countries that previously lacked these concepts, having neither the history nor the political traditions that brought them about. No wonder it seems strange but also familiar to hear of "gays and lesbians" from societies that previously denied having "homosexuality" at all.

One of the great problems of sexual study, particularly of homosexuality, is how many cultures simply lack categories or general concepts that cover the meanings of the contemporary notion of homosexual. We have already seen in the Preface the difficulty that this lack caused me in studying the Sambia. In terms of the ideas and perceptions of many westerners, Sambia men are engaging in homosexual behavior all the time. However, this is not the case from the perspective of the Sambia: They have no idea at all of homoerotic relations between adults, they have an ideal that a man will cease to practice inseminating boys once he becomes a father, and they could not understand the western idea of two men or two women living sexually and socially together throughout their lives. This idea is very alien to the culture; that is why they have no category term *homosexuality!*

For the Sambia and many other cultural traditions, then, people who engage in same-gender relations are acting in the absence of identity terms that commonly circulate in western culture. They may not have the words or concepts to describe how they feel—either because their culture does not register the desires or because they remain isolated or cut off from the appropriate sources of understanding within their own community. Yet their desires and actions make it clear from the perspectives of today that no matter what they have called themselves or the names they have been called, their desiring and loving the same gender are vital parts of their lives. This is why, in the end, we can brave the difficulties of creating concepts that help us to study and compare these sexual cultures.

We can group the necessary concepts into several areas: sexuality, gender, and gay/lesbian. We might think that defining these terms would be easy for the social scientist who makes a living from studying such matters; but the words *sex, love,* and *romance,* among others, have so many meanings, to so many people, under so many circumstances, that they defy easy definition. Or perhaps, as American sociologist John Gagnon (1990) might say, these terms map onto complex, overlapping, and changing "sexual scripts." As the culture changes, Gagnon would argue, so, too, do the scripts, and this in turn results in change in the very concepts circulated and ultimately analyzed by social scientists. And more recently, change in the culture also means change in the intellectual study of sexuality.

From Gay and Lesbian to Queer Studies

Over the last decade a shift has begun to occur in the ideas and values of scholars and citizens who study and read about sexuality. For more than two decades gay and lesbian studies have thrived in the social sciences and humanities as the political power of gays and lesbians progressed in western countries. Most of the work reported in this book, including my own, comes out of this scholarly and popular writing. But in recent years a new voice has risen to nudge and push the older one in a new direction—a sign not only of political and social change in the ideas at play, but also of the aging of a generation of lesbians and gays and the emergence of a new generation of thinkers concerned with same-gender desires and relationships.

We might characterize this shift as a perspectival difference in "gay theory" or "lesbian theory" versus "queer theory." These terms are difficult to focus, and they overlap in many areas. We might think of the contrast like this: Where gays and lesbians were marginalized, queers see themselves in the center, but charged with exposing the forms of power that define normality and manipulate people. The concept of "heteronormal" is the most important notion here since it seeks to interrogate and expose the strong tendency in western culture toward heterosexualism—that is, the chauvinistic assumption that "heterosexuality" as a system of social relations and practices, such as marriage, is the one and only normal and natural way to be human. Previously lesbians and gays sought political power and identities that classified them in a marginal category and, in turn, defined their sexual difference, thus providing them with political and social power much in the way ethnic minorities had achieved "cultural status." Today, however, queers disclaim difference and oppose classifications of all kinds. Where gay and lesbian literature discovered itself by narrating the lived experience of being on the margin or growing up closeted and then coming out, queers shun these attributes in favor of studying and interpreting texts, especially literature and popular culture (Butler 1993; Sedgwick 1990; Lauretis 1993). Queer theory seeks to find the cracks and cleavages between things rather than the things themselves. Where anthropology sought to discover a new culture and history sought to uncover a period of past social life, queer theory seeks the link between these studies. By use of the "deconstruction," or reinterpretation, of texts, queer theorists worry over linkages among epistemology, theory, literature, philosophy, and popular culture.

In lesbian and gay writing, the person/subject—however marginalized—was regarded as whole and unitary, and the struggle of the scholar was to investigate and regain the wholeness of the experience shattered by the secrecy and marginalization of same-gender desires in the past. Gay writing in the fields of history and anthropology and literature thus sought to recover what had been hidden or erased in stories summing up the gay experience. Queer theory, however, argues that history and culture descriptions are never distinguishable from the authors and assumptions of normality through which subjects or objects are described. There is no interest in "sexual identity" and the "body" as such in queer theory since its advocates regard these not as the stable markers of same-gender desires and lives (the very basis of gay and lesbian studies) but as illusions in language and power relationships. No doubt this all sounds a bit abstract and utopian. Where gay and lesbian studies continue a utopian quest, begun at the end of the nineteenth century, of trying to secure freedom and acceptance of gays as "different" but marginal in society, queers go one step further in refusing all classification and all notions of "normality."

Sexual Cultures and Sexual Lifeways

Over the decades anthropologists and other scholars, most notably beginning with Bronislaw Malinowski, Ruth Benedict, and Margaret Mead have articulated several principles about the relationship between culture and sexuality. Four of these concern us here. First, nonwestern societies, past and present, have sexual cultures and codes of sexual practices as complex as our own system of sexuality. Second, sexuality is a part of the social fabric of custom, kinship, and family relations and must be understood in this broader sense of the total social system. Third, sexual variations in behavior are common across human groups, and a high degree of tolerance is accorded to same-gender relations in the majority of societies. This challenges us not to assume but rather to explain the powerful influence of heteronormativity as a social fact in western cultures. Fourth, the accumulation of anthropological knowledge in all societies has enabled us to reflect on the history of sexuality in western culture and to humanize the laws, which historically rendered gays and lesbians outlaws in their own civilization.

Because the power of culture is so great in influencing the social economies and laws of sexuality, it behooves us to study how culture shapes the social perception of reality. Anthropologists believe that to grow up in a culture and to speak its language are so fundamental to the structure of our experience of reality that different cultures can create distinctive realities. This includes not only how people think, and the ways in which they form relationships, but also how they perceive and define physical reality in the time and space world. For instance, the Inuit of Canada grow up with snow and conditions of ice and sleet about which they must be knowledgeable for their survival; thus the Inuit come to perceive minute differences in winter precipitation. They recognize numerous distinctive types of snow and ice, which are named and categorized in their culture. The Inuit have also evolved a more complex gender system that recognizes multiple genders, not simply male and female. In fact, their theory of birth and reincarnation suggests that humans have had past lives as the other gender, and their shamans are routinely understood to be a third gender (d'Anglure 1986). Such an idea may seem fantastical to us; it is. But we must remember that we do not differentiate snow and ice in the same way, and neither do we link the sacred and the sexual with such forces. This raises a general issue that leads back to cultural relativism.

The concept of sexual culture is systematic and must include notions of the whole person and spirituality. A sexual culture is a conventionalized and shared system of sexual practices, supported by beliefs and roles. Far too often in the past, cross-cultural study tended to reduce the meaning of the homoerotic relations to sex acts, and this is wrong. In many of the great nonwestern traditions, sexuality is a part of the social and cosmological fabric, involving kinship, rituals, concepts of the whole person (the rights, obligations and duties of a social position), religious worship, and images of the sacred. These areas indicate a deeper reality, a cultural lifeway, that involves the whole person, gender, and concepts of the local theory of human nature as part of the package of sexuality. Homoerotic desire and relationships are no different. Too often the writing of social science has omitted these deeper, and especially the spiritual areas, of sexuality and homoerotic relations, which are absolutely vital in the many traditions of "two-spirit" persons in Native North America (Roscoe 1991).

As Ruth Benedict argues so eloquently, the spectrum of human cultures is so great, and the range of lifeways so immense in complexity and wisdom, that anyone who bothers to understand variations across cultures is likely to become more tolerant of human diversity. "No man can thoroughly participate in any culture unless he has been brought up and has lived according to its forms, but he can grant to other cultures the same significance to their participants which he recognizes in his own" (Benedict 1934, 37). She continues:

> We have seen that any society selects some segment of the arc of possible human behavior, and in so far as it achieves integration its institutions tend to further the expiation of its selected segment and to inhibit opposite expressions. But these opposite expressions are the congenial responses ... of a certain proportion of the carrier of that cultures. ... We cannot, therefore, even on theoretical grounds imagine that all the congenial responses of all its people will be equally served by the institutions of any culture. To understand the behavior of the individual, it is not merely necessary to relate his personal life-history to his endowments, and to measure these against an arbitrarily selected normality. It is necessary also to relate his congenital response to the behavior that is singled out in the institutions of his culture. (Benedict 1934, 254)

However, far from being accepted in the community or celebrated in the culture for having a special nature, as occurs among American Indians, the lesbian or gay person who desired the same sex typically existed outside of the law and on the margins of our own culture. Of course, many examples of sexual intolerance can be found elsewhere, too. In some societies to love or have sex with another boy or girl, man or woman, is to challenge the conventions of the community and religion, and this may be punished by ostracism or imprisonment and, at the extreme, death. American society has made tremendous strides in the acceptance of homosexuality: People can often live and work openly as gay or lesbian today, have networks of friends, and go about the business of planning a relatively orderly and happy life in many areas because of such changes. But where does this leave us in understanding the lifeways of gays and lesbians around the world?

Sexual Cultures

A growing body of cross-cultural work—primarily historical, anthropological, and sociological—has altered the shape of our understanding of homosexuality, suggesting new theoretical ideas and empirical analyses of same-sex meanings across time and space. Today the term *homosexual* is defined both as a subjective state of individual desire for erotic contact with persons of the same gender and as a significant cultural category of identity involving social, political,

and economic practices and social institutions that are above and beyond individual actors. In this book we must study both dimensions.
We must also be aware that individual desires are largely a matter of
western history and culture, involving the notion of individualism
and the jural individual as elements in liberal democracy. By contrast, the institutions of kinship, family, marriage, and religion transcend individual wishes and do not depend on them for their continuing existence. In fact, the difference in conceptions is crucial for an
understanding of the reluctance of individuals in nonwestern and
eastern cultures to openly identify themselves with sexual identities
that would oppose or make them stand apart from these traditions.

In many cultures around the world it is not possible to talk about
"sex" as a noun or freestanding category of meaning or behavior
separate from the actors and relationships that involve sexuality. It
follows that in many cultures people cannot think about "wanting
sex" or "having sex" or "desiring sex" because there are no ready
culture and language forms that correspond to these agentic ideas.
Likewise, we cannot speak of sexual identities or personalities in
these traditions, as connoted by the western concepts homosexuals
or heterosexuals, lesbians or gay men. To reiterate: These are cul-
ture-bound ideas, and, indeed, they are relatively recent even in the
western tradition—a by-product of the historical transition to the
modern period—with all of its political, economic, and social controls on the sexual nature and sexual culture.

And yet we are reminded of the pervasive presence of persons who
desire the same gender in many places around the world. It is likely
that not only this desire but also the practice of same-gender sexual
relations in one form or another occur in all or nearly all human societies. At the same time, we must not mistake the presence of the
desire or individuals who practice same-gender relations for the acceptance or the institutionalization of the form. Societies vary
greatly in terms of those that approve or disapprove of sexual variations (Carrier 1980; Read 1980). There are those that are more tolerant and may even promote same-gender relations. The Sambia of
New Guinea are an example of numerous Melanesian societies that
practiced boy-inseminating rituals to create manhood. The more
than one hundred American Indian tribes that institutionalized the

two-spirit role, such as the "manly hearted" woman who could serve as a warrior and take a wife, are another of these large traditions (Williams 1986). In one of the most widely cited cross-cultural studies ever published, sociologist Clelland Ford and biologist Frank Beach (1951) found that same-gender sexual relations were considered acceptable and normative in certain people at certain times in the life cycle in 64 percent of the seventy-seven societies studied. In general this suggests that western societies, such as the United States, are what we might call "sex-negative" cultures, which disapprove of sexual variations and have been intolerant specifically of homosexuality. We must not think that this is typical of the range of human groups. Certainly, few societies have systematically forbidden and punished homosexuality as much as have historical western countries over the past century (Greenberg 1988). If a person has homoerotic desires, it is better to grow up in a "sex-positive" tradition, such as those in Polynesia, which still has its own biases and sexual stigmas (Besnier 1994).

But saying this is not the same thing as saying that homosexuality is universal or might be found in all human groups. Why not? The cultural and linguistic specificity of the term *homosexuality,* a concept of history and culture, has rather precise specifications for what should occur. What the idea now connotes to many westerners goes beyond its original meaning, however: that homosexuality is a sexual orientation based on innate biological drives or agencies. Such a notion, already circulated in the growing popularity of the idea of a "gay brain," is entirely a matter of speculation, though one that has its attractions. But another meaning of homosexuality that makes it impossible to establish as a universal is the idea that homoerotic conduct will occur throughout the life of the person. Such a pattern, as we have seen, is rare by the standards of societies around the world. Today, however, the traits of biological innateness, sexual exclusivity of erotic behavior, lifelong adherence to same-gender relations, and self-identification with a social category are all implied by the general terms *homosexual/heterosexual* and *gay/lesbian/straight* and are very difficult to identify outside of the western tradition.

In Chapter 4 we study examples of life-crisis rituals and coming of age ceremonies as processes that correspond to the period in which people "come out" in our own culture. These are not the same, of course, but they invite comparison. These processes include hiding, passing, coming out—which celebrate the cultural ways of being lesbian or gay in a variety of cultures, including our own. Some of these same individuals go on in later life to actively self-identify as homosexual, bisexual, or lesbian/gay. But many never do so for a variety of reasons—including the societal norm to marry, the social imperative to carry on the family line, and the desire to have children, which in many cultures are regarded as a source of social prestige and genuine happiness in their own right. Taboos exist within the social groups, religious communities, or tribes regarding the punishment of homosexuality, and these pose a terrible barrier to self-identification and "coming out" as lesbian or gay for those who would like to do so. Money, in this regard, is one of the last great social barriers to coming out in the western nations, as demonstrated by the virtual absence of prominent gay and lesbian individuals in the great moneyed families of the United States. In fact, the reasons that people conform to or rebel against all social rules, especially sexual ones, are usually complicated. Perhaps they have compromised their same-gender desires through what poet Adrienne Rich (1980) once called "compulsory heterosexuality," or they have taken on heterosexuality as a "compromise formation" in the assumed "normal" development of personality, as feminist psychoanalyst Nancy Chodorow (1992) suggests. Compromise adjustments, such as a marriage of convenience, may be relatively easy to make in many cases, but they are painful to live and difficult to undo; society has a long memory, and people would rather pretend or look the other way so as to avoid having their beliefs and assumptions about "normal heterosexuality" challenged. A "conspiracy of silence" often reigns in this domain of human relations. Moreover, people can change and develop desires (a woman desiring another woman over her husband) where previously none was apparent, thus perplexing themselves and causing consternation to others. Understanding these pressures and possibilities teaches tolerance and provides compassion for the diversity of sexual lifeways found in all societies.

Some authorities have wondered how much Christianity, Judaism, and Islam have instilled negative attitudes about homosexuality. Although the answers are inconclusive, they generally tend to support the idea that heterosexualism and power hierarchies of all kind derive at least some of their force from organized religion. (For a review of some of the religion and homosexuality literature, see Greenberg 1988; Herdt 1987a.)

The late John Boswell (1980), a noted gay historian, showed that in the late Roman Empire there was no general classification that separated same-gender desires or people who would today be called "gay or lesbian" from others in society, at least in the main urban centers of the empire. Boswell also believed that the early Roman Catholic Church did not oppose homosexuality or regard it as unnatural, although some authorities take a different view (Greenberg 1988). Certainly, the early Roman Catholic Church did not go out of its way to penalize or punish anyone simply because of his or her sexual practices. Only later, following profound changes in ecclesiastical policy after the eleventh century, did a negative and lasting change emerge. No one knows exactly why; perhaps this change had to do with the increasing visibility of the minorities of the time and the prominence of the Jews in the rhetoric of the Crusades. Or perhaps it was the result of the waning power of the church and the rise of the great imperial states in Europe, beginning with Portugal, Spain, Holland, and France, which created new contests for property between religious and secular leaders and led to a vilification of all sexuality, especially any conduct that might drain the church of its wealth or its prestige. The formation of the Inquisition, which linked heresy, devil worship, and sodomy for centuries, was devastating, and it is easy to speculate that the image of the sodomite as an evil being is a historical product of those centuries. Nevertheless, the Reformation did not automatically alter the situation in predictable ways, which suggests that antihomosexual imagery has had other sources in the transition to modernity (Van der Meer 1994). Whatever the case, we can be sure that religion has played a prime role in western attitudes about homosexuality, but it is not sufficient to explain the intensely negative antihomosexual ideas that came into being in the modern period or the persistence today of such powerful sexual prejudice (Young-Bruehl 1996).

Comparative study therefore demonstrates that forms of homosexuality known from ancient times are related to the historical and cultural conditions of human development, oppression, freedom, and adaptation. Because of the difficulty of comparing forms of same-gender relations across time and space, it is useful to create an analytical construct that is not dependent on western definitions of sexuality. Such a concept is "sexual culture," which describes a consensual model of cultural ideals about sexual behavior in a group. A sexual culture suggests a worldview based on specific sexual and gender norms, emotions, beliefs, and symbolic meanings regarding the proper nature and purpose of sexual encounters. Sexual cultures thus function as powerful systems of moral and emotional control; notions of honor and shame as they relate to sexual behavior are especially notable in the creation of masculinity and male prowess or submission. Sexual honor refers to what is "normal, natural, necessary, or approved" in a community or an individual. Sexual socialization brings on these subjectivities, with their means of suggesting what is shameful or honorable in every sexual encounter. Thus, an adult New Guinea man (or a Greek man) must never be the one who is penetrated, only the penetrator; and certain heterosexual men who prefer the so-called missionary position (the man on top, the woman on the bottom, in coitus) cannot bear the idea of the woman being on top, for this submission would shame or dishonor them. The effectiveness of these ideas and emotions is evidenced by the strength with which sanctions are levied to punish those who violate the norms. Sexual cultures thus include and exclude large areas of human ideas and feelings, generally supporting the systems of power and status in the larger historical surround.

In this way sexual cultures always teach standards regarding gender, and it is impossible to analyze sexual cultures without looking into the gendered relationships they create between people. The culture teaches the role of man or woman as an honorable sexual position, filled with feeling and power. Gender mediates these norms since customary patterns of masculinity and femininity—exhibited through roles, task assignments, social status, and exchange systems—influence the expression of many sexual practices. Homosexuality seems particularly vulnerable to systems of repressive sexuality; in many countries power systems that suppress the rights, feelings, and agency of women (sexism) are also prone to suppress the desires, feelings, and agency of gays and lesbians (homophobia). Thus, in many traditions around the world it is not the gender of the sexual partner that matters so much as the sexual behavior that occurs between individuals. In Mexico (Carrier 1995), for instance, the notion of being penetrated is a slander on a man's reputation and may result in social catastrophe. But Mexican men in the barrio accept the notion of penetrating a social inferior in order to achieve sexual pleasure. And in Nicaragua the nexus between emasculation and homosexuality seems especially clear among revolutionary Sandinista men. As men attempted to create gender equality and curtail machismo (the assertion of phallic masculinity), many began to fear that they would all turn into queers because of their softness (Lancaster 1995).

In modern western history the category of the homosexual originates primarily from late-nineteenth-century notions, derived from medicine, that defined same-sex desire as the product of disease, degeneracy, and moral inversion. These notions created an image of a woman trapped in a man's body or of a male body with a female brain—a third sex apart from the rest of humanity. Not only did this cultural image foster increasing prejudice in the effort to reform sexual laws (Weeks 1985), but it also produced some of the strongest trappings of homophobia, many of which live on today. Surely the appeal of Magnus Hirschfeld, the German homosexual doctor who led the first emancipation movement a century ago, cannot be understood apart from the idea that the third sex, "intermediate sex," or "sexual invert" was a person who had been born this way and could not change. Hirschfeld, like other sexual reformers of the time, hoped that such an ideology would serve to relax the antihomosexual laws in Germany. In fact, of course, this ideology may have paved the way for the Holocaust as a "final solution" to the homosexual problem (Plant 1989).

In fact, the invention of cultural symbols that aim to seize on and transform the horrors of homophobia and holocaust has emerged from this history. The famous "pink triangle" is such a symbol of the gay and lesbian sexual culture today. It comes down to us as a historical legacy of the killing of millions of Jews and untold numbers of homosexuals, including homosexual Jews, by the Nazis in World War II. The icon connotes the pride of speaking out and of never forgetting the cost of silence among those who celebrate love of the same gender in contemporary western society. It is through symbols of this kind that we come to see what is at stake in the invention of the sexual identity systems homosexual/heterosexual and their appropriation as memorials of global gay culture.

Increasingly, the evidence of anthropology demonstrates the existence of a division between "homosexuality" in nonwestern/premodern societies and same-sex relations found in contemporary western European/North American societies. In short, research argues against the idea of a universal category of homosexuality in individual development. Here we might lean toward the "social constructionist" side of the debate on the causes of sexual orientations and lifeways. What we have reviewed thus far suggests that sharing the distinctive cultural identity of being homosexual or gay/lesbian is typical only of autonomous individual agents known from western societies in the late twentieth century. But what can we say about the function of "essentialism" in these debates? How are we to explain the apparent existence of persons who desire relations with the same gender in great numbers of traditions across time and space, even when they have never heard of the concept of homosexuality?

Comparing Sexual Lifeways

Cultural study in nonwestern societies stresses the importance of examining not only the environment in which same-gendered relations occur, but also the symbolic systems of beliefs, rules, norms, and social exchanges surrounding sexuality. A sexual culture creates strong attitudes and beliefs about the approved and disapproved forms of sexual relations in a society. It suggests not only what should be desired and sought in life, but also what should be avoided and forbidden. To speak of sexual "identity" or "orientation" or "preference" in this area of human life is probably misleading. Not only does it strongly imply that a conscious, intentional choice has been made—

an idea that opposes much of what we know about the development of sexuality. It also runs aground culturally because sexual desires are not so easily learned in the body, like individual tastes for pickled herring and Beethoven. A sexual identity implies a system of preferences based on morally laden cultural ideas and emotions of what is valued and desired by the *society as a whole*. In this context sexual identity is not the product solely of what individuals might prefer. Such a system of culturally prescribed preferences is as much a source of opposition, or a site of cultural resistance, as it is of learning. Certainly, if the matter of sexual preferences could be reduced to learning, we would not expect to find many homosexuals in the western tradition since antihomosexual imagery is so profound, a point of view supported by psychoanalytic thinkers from Freud to Robert Stoller (1985). In short, a different notion is required, one that is deeper, but also more collective, than preference. To contrast and compare the sexual cultures of the world, and to make sense of their patterns, I use the concept of sexual lifeways.

By sexual lifeways, I mean the specific erotic ideas and emotions, categories and roles, that constitute individual development within a particular sexual culture. These lifeways can be broken down into component forms, most of them gendered according to whether one is male or female or third gender. Here a wealth of symbolic devices and social practices is absorbed along with language in a way that is more subtle than simple conscious learning, but also includes the embodiment of desires. When a pattern, such as touching, is experienced early and often in life, is reinforced by norms about sexual touching and the emotions of holding or withholding touch, and is then expressed in a variety of gender and sexual relations, such an area of subjective culture is part of one's body and being. By socializing individuals into culturally shared images of these sexual lifeways, the culture is able to influence the very perception of the body and its symbolism as expressed in gender, marriage, and reproduction and the creation of emotions in sexual desires and social traditions. Sexual lifeways can endure throughout a lifetime and bring the full weight of social tradition into the desire for sexual fulfillment. This is the sense in which I would suggest that sexuality and culture are the very essence of what makes our species both distinctive and given to sexual exploration and diversity in the doings of sexuality. Many other animal species have sex and plenty of it; indeed, some of them more than us. But humans are alone among them in having symbolic institutions that create meaning and purpose in life beyond reproduction, in how erotic desire and relations define the fabric of culture. When we engage in sexual relations, we are contributing once more to the creation and recreation of a whole cultural world—its mythology and intentional design of reality.

The cultural classification of sexual lifeways provides for sex assignment and socialization into normatively arranged masculine, feminine, and androgynous roles. This is the province of gender. The gendered course of life as a pathway of development from childhood through old age is instrumental in this framework. People in western culture learn early and quickly what is regarded as boyish and girlish and in between. Gender identity, the sense of maleness or femaleness, and in some traditions the sense of being a third sex, is critical here—a core of subjectivity that embodies the desires of the larger tradition. Contained within these gendered practices, as well as the sexual lifeways that express them, are deeply motivating notions of arousal and lust; dread and taboo; excitement and eros; emotional gendered subjective states, such as honor and shame; and perceptions of objects, particularly other bodies, including fetishes, but also other things, including gods, that move the person toward desire and fulfillment. Each sexual lifeway and each sexual culture stipulate a local theory of human nature and sexual nature as well as the conditions for the achievement of full personhood and reproductive and sexual competence. Such a total system of values provides for a more satisfying analysis of same-gender eros, desires, and practices across time and space.

In the pages that follow we read of many cultures with an eye toward understanding how historical and cultural conditions have enabled or suppressed basic human desires. Nonwestern societies are typically more tolerant of variations across the spectrum of sexual behavior, and in some cases they are more tolerant of departures from sexual norms, depending on context and the actor's ability to achieve cultural ideals. By contrast, western cultures since the early modern period have been more disapproving and punishing of all variations in the domains of sexuality and gender, especially of homosexuality. No doubt this has much to do with how sexual identity has become a permanent identity marker that separates the individual from the group in the western tradition. We study the reasons later, but one seems to be that same-gender relations violate the historical western cultural ideals of what is morally proper human nature or, to be more precise, "sexual nature." Here we may see at work the expression of very old, even ancient ideas that derive from the Judeo-Christian worldview and have been combined with notions of sex as "sin" and sex as "disease" when it comes to same-gender relations.

In many western countries, for example, the preferential cultural ideal is for sex to occur only in monogamous marriage and only for the purpose of having children; deviations from this norm may be punished, however mildly, as wrong. Sexual socialization in many western cultures is surrounded by idioms of sexual nature and biological lore; suggestive moralistic notions about why things should be done in a certain way, even because of biological evolution; and warnings of the dire consequences should sex taboos be broken. These ideals typically are more restrictive for women than for men, since dominant male hegemonies prescribe the "double standard" of monogamy for women and extramarital relations, including same-gender illicit relations with other males, for their husbands.

These are the ideas to be explored in this book. But I should interject a note about the cases to which we turn. The archives of anthropology, even though limited in the understanding of homosexuality, are still very large, and I could not possibly represent all cultures and peoples in this small book. Instead, my goal is to provide scope—variation, complexity, and some sense of the lived experience of particular cultures—but without exhaustively covering all cases. For instance, we examine in more detail the lessons provided by the Sambia people of the Highlands of New Guinea, with whom I have lived for many years. We compare the Sambia to other sexual cultures of the Southwest Pacific that institutionalize ritual insemination practices of boys in order to grow and masculinize them into strong warriors. To facilitate the presentation of the cross-cultural cases, I use a model that takes into account five widely agreed on forms of same-gender relations around the world. These forms are (1) age-structured relations as the basis for homoerotic relationships between older and younger males, (2) gender-transformed homoerotic roles that allow a person to take the sex/gender role of the other gender, (3) social roles that permit or require the expression of same-gender relations as a particular niche in society, (4) western homosexuality as a nineteenth-century form of sexual identity, and (5) late-twentieth-century western egalitarian relationships between persons of the same gender who are self-consciously identified as gay or lesbian for all of their lives.

◀ 2 ▶

Cultural Myths About Homosexuality

ONE OF THE OLDEST OF ALL MYTHS in the modern western tradition is that homosexuality is evil: a sin, a disease, and a crime, whether against society or against nature; an abnormal lifeway that creates hypersexual and selfish delinquents, fiendish vampires, and monsters on the edge of society. This imagery is so filled with nonsense and prejudice that to reasoned people it looks ridiculous. Yet many areas of cultural history are antiquated, dehumanizing, and filled with false notions of this kind. And whatever new myths about being gay or lesbian emerge to replace this distorted imagery, we can be sure that they will also contain the cultural reasoning of history and society, however true or false. But while other forms of prejudice have ebbed, homophobia has endured, and intense hatred of same-gender relations, even among peaceful and kind people, seems a mystery that invites investigation.

The stories of evil homosexuality are a confusion of many things: of the homosexual with disease, of sinning with sexual desire, of gay life with what is unnatural. Might this not also represent the suspicions of ignorant folk who confuse being exceptional with being abnormal? Surely there have been many great human beings who desired the same gender, but we need not list them again here, for we are concerned with the average citizen of society, with the same right to be exceptional and gay. Let us try to unpack these myths by reviewing a few simple points.

25

A word of caution, however: We should not think that merely by proving the existence of same-gender desires and practices in other cultures, we will be able to disprove these stereotypes and prejudices. Magic, one realizes, cannot be disproved. And bigotry (a form of magical thinking) remains stubbornly planted in closed minds, even when we can show that other cultures do things differently, even better. The world has seen much bigotry posing as morality, even myth posing as science. But the prejudice against homosexuality continues and must never be underestimated; it is one of the most destructive forces of our time.

Most of us know the difference among belief, myth, and science. Myths are timeless social realities and change ever so slowly. Belief exists independent of proof in the time and space world, though individuals can unlearn their beliefs and discover new realities. It is difficult to disprove the magical belief that being gay or lesbian is unnatural or evil. Myth, however, draws its existence from a collective pool of beliefs and stories that transcend individuals, and myths mask the structures and historical prerogatives of power in societies. Perhaps we can at least unmask the false and spurious assumptions on which antique myths are founded by replacing them with new social realities that are more positive and productive of the lives of gay and lesbian people.

Science is not always a certain ally in this change, for science is itself a part of society, and its own positions and perspectives on reality are not foolproof. The social sciences, like the biological sciences, are no different in this respect, although we have seen much progress in the ability of dedicated scholars to poke enough holes in the faulty use of science that we are able to move onto higher ground. That is the aim of this chapter: to clear the air about historical misunderstandings and cultural prejudices against homosexuality. The goal in studying the cross-cultural record is to understand the range of sexual lifeways, which include same-gender relationships, in the majority of societies. If we cannot establish the "naturalness" of same-gender desires, we can at least see that some people who have lived their lives loving the same gender are special and gifted, with unusual talents, intuitions, and creative powers. Or they may be quite ordinary and average, people who happen to desire the same gender but are like everybody else in all other ways. Such is the messy and wonderful character of life, a source of wisdom to cherish.

The most important lesson to learn from the cross-cultural and historical study of homosexuality is that there is room for many at the table of humankind in societies around the world. The mistake of modern western culture, however, is to continue the legalization of prejudice against lesbians and gays. Even though racial and religious prejudice is largely illegal and seldom tolerated in public affairs, all too often demagogues continue to profit from antigay rhetoric and sociopolitical discrimination on a wide range of fronts, from job discrimination, to prohibition on lesbian and gay marriage, to adoption of children by same-gender couples who would make good parents (Patterson 1995).

Since my own society, the United States, is one of the battlegrounds on which these issues have been, and are still being, fought, let me first say a word about my own culture. Americans are constantly confronted with a shameful history of homophobia and antigay legislation stretching back into the early modern period (D'Emilio and Freedman 1988). The American worldview, much like the European, defined homosexuality as a sin and later as a disease. Americans in the last century regarded the sexual "invert" as a sign of decay and moral chaos, much as they did feminism and the women's emancipation movement. Medical and scientific authorities as well as the general public believed that inverts were degenerates in personality or spirit. At one time or other, every imaginable ill and moral corruption were blamed on same-gender desire. The dirty, the beastly and monstrous, the ungodly and impure, the satanic and evil—such labels and metaphors were widespread and imputed to the person who desired the same gender. All western nations share in this historical legacy, though some of them, such as Holland, have parted with it and made amends, as noted in Chapter 5. But in those that have not done so, these labels are still in circulation and pose quite terrible barriers to the process of "coming out" among younger men and women (Herdt and Boxer 1996)—an issue to which I return and devote more attention in Chapter 4.

But the times are changing, and although all is not perfect today, we Americans are an optimistic people who live in a world of increasing enlightenment, and the tolerance for homosexuality is definitely growing, at least in the public opinion polls (Laumann et al. 1994). Today it is possible as never before for youths to come out and anticipate living lives of relative freedom as gay or lesbian in our society. This does not mean that bigotry is gone or that battles regarding gays in the military and gay and lesbian marriages will not be fought for years to come. However, some of the old stereotypes about evil homosexuality are now openly ridiculed in the media, and these may seem ludicrous to some readers, until, that is, we recall the terrible incidents of recent years: the fact that the AIDS epidemic was initially blamed on gay men, the victimization of lesbians who would like to have children, or the loss by lesbian mothers of their younger children, who have been taken away by the courts, among other issues that remain contentious. Such is the painful record on the human rights of lesbians and gay men in the United States.

As an indication of change, we might consider the opinion of Freud. Even the great make mistakes. For even though Freud's ([1905] 1962) understanding of sexuality as generalizably bisexual and "polymorphously perverse" (open-ended, pleasure seeking) opened the way for an enlightened expansion of the concept of the sexual in western culture, on the matter of homosexuality Freud was contradictory and initially biased. However, over the course of some forty years the founder of psychoanalysis and this remarkable student of sexual nature changed his own views, disavowing his formerly negative ideas—that homosexuality was everything from narcissism to schizophrenia. He seemed to realize in the end the harm that his view had done. Freud's last advice in 1935 is helpful even today. Homosexuality is admittedly "no virtue," Freud stated, but neither is it a "vice or a disease." Freud seemed to suggest that, far from feeling shame over the matter, people should learn to accept their same-gender desires. As Robert Stoller (1985) later added: Gays and lesbians should make the most of life, including full use of their creativity as well as of the enhanced compassion for suffering in others and appreciation for happiness that the struggle to overcome bigotry can bring. Where once it was impossible to be open about these matters, today noted gay psychoanalyst Richard Isay (1996) writes eloquently of the possibilities of the gay man or lesbian creating positive self-affirmation and loving same-gender relations in America.

Morality and Normality

Two points should be underlined to start. First, do not be fooled by cultural rhetoric about the causes of homosexuality, which assumes that same-gender desires are a problem to be fixed. Second, never confuse "morality" with "normality" in these debates. In the first case, all such arguments suggest the removal of homosexuality as a thorn in the side of society. We must always remain critical about the underlying assumptions of such ideas about "human nature." In the second case, all concepts of normality are cultural and historically situated definitions of sexual lifeways. Because the "sexual" and "gender" are so subject to cultural symbols, as Freud (1905) hinted and Stoller (1985) later confirmed in the area of sexual subjectivity, there is considerable plasticity in the ability of humans to adapt themselves to each sexual culture. And as we have already seen, not only is there great variability across cultures, but also even within the same society social change in sexuality and gender is a necessary part of the human condition. Therefore, it is inaccurate and narrow-minded to believe that there is any uniform and unchanging concept of sexual morality and normality around the world. These are important indications of what has come out of cultural study in recent years.

The heavy moralizing about sexuality in general and homosexuality in particular that is to be found in western countries today, especially the United States, seems to be a product of another historical era. It hints that all sex should be for reproduction and that pleasure is wrong. In past centuries the pressure on population and the religious control of sexuality may have well determined such attitudes, but those influences are antiquated, although perhaps not entirely gone. We might think of this as a kind of reproductive logic that capitalizes on traditional Judeo-Christian morality.

Surely this old morality cannot be explained purely as a result of religious faith or worship, though religious beliefs have certainly been among the most powerful factors shaping the continued homophobia in western society. In the sexual culture of the past, the emphasis on having children was constant and defined the roles of men and women in many respects. As noted American historian Carroll Smith-Rosenberg (1985, 47) has written of the times, "Gender distinctions were rooted in biology, and so, therefore, was the patriarchal world order." There was a general fear of sexuality that seems very strange to our present view. Only men were supposed to have lust and biological "sex drives," while women were supposedly more maternal and pure, responding to popular culture ideas such as "maternal instincts" and "love drives." As historians such as Paul Robinson (1976), Smith-Rosenberg (1985), and Jeffrey Weeks (1985) have so well reported, "normal" and "morally proper" relationships between men and women were fraught with conflict and contradiction, such as the idea that men expected their wives to be pure but also to enjoy (or at least to allow the men to enjoy) sexual pleasure. Homosexuals and inverts were a threat to this regime, perhaps because they symbolized the open embrace of passion and sexual freedom. Such desires and ideas go against the old social control of women and definitely against the grain of Puritanism, fundamentalist religion, and reproductivity in western civilization.

The most destructive effect of the old rhetoric of sin and degeneracy is the treatment of homosexuality as a "problem" to fix or a "flaw" to remove. Out of sight, as the old saying goes, is out of mind. The abnormal/disease rhetoric thus seeks to locate a cause for "what went wrong" with the homosexual in order to "fix, repair, or cure it." Take note, however, that the best scientific reviews of the last twenty years have concluded that no evidence exists to support the idea that someone can be "cured" through medical or psychological treatment of his or her same-gender desires (Murphy 1992). I believe that Freud would have scoffed at the idea that homoerotic desires and attractions can be removed by "sexual conversion" or religious conversion "therapies," which advocate that a person live as Christian and heterosexual, "make a choice" for God or for heterosexuality, and deny same-gender relationships (including friendships). Not only is there no sound evidence to support the claims of such therapies, but also there is good reason to question their ethics and the damage they may do to people's lives (Haldeman 1994).

We seek to repair or replace only what we believe to be "damaged" or "bad," and this may well continue be the basis for attitudes about the treatment of homosexuality. Indeed, the public continues to be enthralled by the latest headlines about THE CAUSE of homosexuality—claims about genes or hormones or parents or whatever. It is unlikely that such a cause will ever be found, given the incredible complexity of sexual identity development, cultural contexts of desires and relationships, and the individual differences that exist in and between people who are gay, lesbian, and/or bisexual (Herdt 1990; Stoller and Herdt 1985).

Some of the heavy moralizing that surrounds homosexuality as an issue has to do with the question of whether people "choose" to desire the same gender. If it is a choice, then (so the logic goes) people can choose not to do it. This folk concept of normal sexuality of course favors a person having a heterosexual life. Proponents of this view never question whether heterosexuality is a choice in the same way. In fact, most self-identified heterosexuals find themselves attracted to the other gender at such an early age that they cannot think of their sexual behavior as the result of being a "choice"— their desires feel more like a part of their ontology or sexual nature (Bem 1996). The same kind of experience is widely reported for present-day gay and lesbian adolescents (Herdt and Boxer 1996)— the first generation that could begin to live its desires early in development without as much compromise as before.

This concept of sexual desire or orientation as a "choice" relies on some dubious assumptions and is expressed through cultural stereotypes that are misleading in regard to sexual identity development. What is "free will"? No one imagines that a person chooses eye color or genes, right-handedness or left-handedness. In the castles of their daydreams, philosophers may choose in this way, but for most of the rest of us, life is more a matter of what we feel to be part of our reality, whether it comes from inside of us or from the surrounding society. We can no more choose our reality than we can choose to change our hair color or switch from the right to the left hand.

Oh, yes, we can artificially color our hair, but it will grow back soon enough in the original color; and we can become ambidextrous if we have to, but we will never enjoy using the new hand as much. Questions such as these are endlessly intriguing for moral, political, and philosophical reasons. In the area of sex and law, in particular, as U.S. judge Richard Posner (1992) has noted in his critique of American law and sexuality, questions of sexual "choice" are perplexing and typically misunderstood. Why should the homosexual's private life—erotic desires—not be left alone from social interference, he asks? Posner advises a "hands-off" policy by the government in the area of same-sex laws because "free will" is not what is at stake. It is individual rights and liberties that need to be protected, and sexual orientation and homosexuality are no different, he reasons. In fact, as we know from psychoanalysis, there is little reason to believe that people consciously choose their sexuality or their desires (Stoller 1979). For most of us, our sexual desires are as inevitable and obvious as the color of the sky or the taste of sea water.

Political moralists and religious fundamentalists, in contrast, believe that since people choose their sexuality, they can overcome or "grow" out of the "phase" of "acting out their homosexual problems" and instead marry and have children. The Roman Catholic Church takes a slightly different position since it accepts that some people are born with same-gender desires. However, the church requires them to choose not to act those desires out and instead to get married or remain celibate. The church thus distinguishes between "unnatural" desires and sexual feelings for the same gender, which exist, and the expression of these same tabooed desires in sexual action, which is a sin and is not tolerated. Only the *expression* of desires constitutes a sin—but still a very bad one. Some priests, now openly gay, reject this distinction (Wolf 1989).

Political and religious moralists opposed to homosexuality invariably confuse the different cultural forms of same-gender desire. They confuse and lump together the nineteenth-century "homosexual" who was generally hidden from society and could not lead a normal social life with the twentieth-century "lesbian" or "gay man" who is able to be more open and fully expects to live a normal social life. Such confusion leads to spurious classifications and comparisons, such as the notorious "Don't ask, don't tell," policy of the Pentagon and the American military. This policy is based on the stereotype that all gays and lesbians, unless laws control them, are hypersexual and unable to control their own desires when they are living in close proximity to peers and comrades in barracks. In fact, many countries, such as Canada, Israel, and Australia, already have policies that have gays in the military, and there is no evidence to support such stereotypes (Herek et al. 1996). Sophisticated moralists understand that gays who hide are not the worry; gays and lesbians who wish to live their own lives and be a part of society raise an alarm to those who would not like to examine their assumptions about sexuality or have their own lifeways questioned. By coming out, gay men and lesbians have elected to construct a social world based on the politics of social change and progressive moral activism, which requires choosing *not to hide* as a means of creating and advancing their own community.

These sexual stereotypes are signs of what we should call, in anthropological terms, sexual chauvinism. This notion is based on the idea of ethnocentrism, which is the interpretation of other people's behaviors and customs through the lens of one's own. Where ethnocentrism is ultimately the refusal to understand another way of life, chauvinism is the belief that one's own culture or lifeway is inherently superior to all others. In fact, chauvinists are seldom as reflective as this, more typically reacting rather than thinking about their own perceptions and responses. Sexual chauvinism is a special form of privileging as superior one's sexual lifeways over those of other people. Much of the colonial history of the West is littered with stories of sexual chauvinism, as we see in Chapter 3. Within our own society, however, moralists and fundamentalists espouse sexual chauvinism in the perpetuation of nineteenth-century sexual stereotypes of the kind under discussion. They imagine a world of "family values" that dates from an earlier golden age of heterosexualism. This fiction imagines a world pure of homosexuality, and all other sexual variations, with more traditional gender roles—women as mothers and men as breadwinners.

Why are proponents of this fictional account so frightened of homosexuality, we might ask? Certainly, it cannot be because of the numbers since sexual moralists today claim that there are not many homosexuals. Heterosexuals are, after all, the vast majority. One possible explanation for this fear is that a growing number of self-identified heterosexuals are themselves increasingly dissatisfied with being classified as "heterosexual." It is not that they are unattracted to the other gender; rather, it is that they do not like the traditional values or find them too restrictive for the kind of social and economic world in which we live. Women and men pursue their own careers and jobs, claim their own rights, seek equality and mutuality in their romantic and sexual relations, and this may be threatening to the traditional moralists. New generations who self-identify as straight or queer or bisexual are put on the defensive by the moralism; increasingly they also refuse to be silenced by the attack on gays (Herdt and Boxer 1996).

In a general way the findings of the previously mentioned gay/lesbian adolescent study in Chicago support these points—and also reveal the possibilities of heterosexuals becoming accepting and moving away from sexual chauvinism (Boxer, Cook, and Herdt 1991). Parents of lesbians and gay men in Chicago initially had a difficult time accepting that their children were gay or lesbian. In the most extreme cases, they severed relations with the children, and in a small number of families, an adolescent gay, on discovery, was actually thrown out of the home by the parents. Most families were much more accepting than this, however, and some had virtually no difficulty in accepting the knowledge. Nearly all the parents, however, experienced the news of the children's homosexuality with a sense of loss. Sometimes this was followed by feelings of anger, rage, grief, and, finally (sometimes years later), acceptance of the change. The parents who felt the loss most acutely had the sense that their child—previously identified as heterosexual—was gone or even dead. These parents often expressed the feeling that they would never fulfill their dreams of having grandchildren.

These parents, we have found, bring two powerful assumptions to the question most frequently put to us: "Why is my child gay?" First, they typically assumed that if their child was homosexual, then "something was wrong, and it should be fixed." They immediately wanted their child to go into treatment to become normal. Second, if something went wrong, then they felt that they might have caused what happened. Such feelings are easily manipulated by negative and moralistic rhetoric of the kind just discussed. All of this, however, seems to be driven by the cultural idea that homosexuality is evil or bad, that someone is to blame, and that the blame has to be expunged through the homosexuality being "fixed." Fortunately, the loving and positive families overcame these reactions and eventually developed positive regard for their openly gay sons and lesbian daughters. Some parents even expressed gratitude that they had had their own beliefs—sexual chauvinism—challenged because they grew and learned from the process, finding more positive and accepting relations than they had ever experienced in their families.

Since the time of the Enlightenment, our knowledge of sexual variations in the human condition has slowly increased. Anthropological studies have helped to broaden our understanding of the variations while critically examining the prejudices of western culture in the modern period (Malinowski 1929; Martin 1987; Mead 1935; reviewed in Herdt 1994; Vance 1991). As anthropologist Ruth Benedict (1938) once stated in her illustration of ritual homosexuality in New Guinea, all sexual practices are relative to cultural group and context. Sexuality and sexual meanings vary like language itself, and mere variation is not grounds for the clinical diagnosis of "abnormality."

The lessons of cross-cultural study help to move us beyond sexual chauvinism. To desire the same sex, to be in love with someone of the same gender, or to have sexual relations with such a person is in some cultures to act within the tradition and in others to go beyond the boundaries of kinship and marriage arrangements. Sometimes same-gender relationships are forbidden; rarely are they punished in nonwestern societies as severely as they once were in our own. The record of cross-cultural research demonstrates that same-gender sexuality is tolerated, if not in fact approved, for some persons at some point in their lifetimes in certain societies (Greenberg 1988).

Typically, a society that approves of sexual play and experimentation with both genders in childhood is more open and less punishing in adulthood, especially so long as the adult marries and parents. Much of adult sexuality is defined in tradition-bound societies by the requirement to marry and the imperative to have children. These social demonstrations of kinship and social reproduction should not be confused, however, with sexuality and the life cycle of sexual behavior. Cultures can be more open and less restrictive about premarital and extramarital relations so long as they are handled discreetly; and adolescent experimentation in love and sex with both genders is very common in societies around the world. Sexually tolerant societies and cultures in which same-gender relations are approved tend to provide more flexibility in the range of sexual lifeways all through the stages of growing up and living as an adult, even into old age.

Another peculiar myth that we should address directly concerns the idea that homosexuality originated in the West and was then exported to colonial lands in prior centuries. The former Soviet Union once claimed this; and so did communist Cuba (Lumsden 1996). Such an idea in its rudiment appears as ridiculous as the basic stereotype of homosexuality in the western historical imagination. This myth is found in some nonwestern countries of the world, which contend that homosexuality does not exist in their land. For a variety of reasons, including lack of evidence on sexual behavior in these cultures, the claim is difficult for the western scholar to dispute. The idea that traditional cultures have no homoerotic behavior is contradicted by historical reports, but these, too, are rejected by nationalists and ideologues as being either the product of colonization or the invention of colonial scholars, themselves the pawns of the degeneration of colonialism or capitalism. This is a dubious claim, as we see in Chapter 3, for as Margaret Mead (1961) once advised, we should be very skeptical of claims made for the absence of sexual customs—including homosexuality—when no evidence is offered in support of the claim.

I recall a humorous story told by Igor Kon (1995), the noted Russian sociologist of sexuality. Kon has said that neither East nor West seemed to like sex, and both wanted to disclaim it during the Cold War. The Soviets claimed that sex was a capitalist plot and should not have occurred in Mother Russia. The Americans in the days of the crazed Senator Joseph McCarthy claimed that sex was a communist plot. McCarthy went so far as to accuse Alfred Kinsey, the noted American sex researcher, of communist sympathies, because of Kinsey's findings that many American boys had engaged in casual same-gender sexual relations while growing up. Americans launched a witch hunt for communists and homosexuals—who were, for a time, interchangeable monsters. The Soviets did similar things. Both sides hated homosexuality. Political ideologues, it seems, are not very comfortable with sex and seem especially uncomfortable with the idea that same-gender relations might have been part of the original scheme of things. But we know that politics makes strange bedfellows! The lesson is that hypersexuality is always attributed to the Other—whether another culture or another sexual orientation.

Consider Africa, a huge continent of many diverse cultures, where certain authorities as well as some Africans themselves have claimed that homosexuality did not exist in precolonial times and that it was brought in by the European colonial powers. Remarks that reflect this idea can be heard on the streets of Dakar (Teunis 1996) as well as in some of the great treasures of African literature, such as Marise Condé's *Ségou*. But such claims are disputed by the facts.

The best-known example of precolonial same-gender relations on the African continent is probably the report of anthropologist E. E. Evans-Pritchard (1970) on age-structured homoerotic relationships between older and younger males of the Azande tribe. Restrictions on marriage and the role of the warrior more broadly made marriage complicated and promoted the practice of a man taking a younger male (aged twelve to twenty) as a "court" lover; in fact, Evans-Pritchard refers to the practice as a "marriage." Azande males formed a tightly knit homosocial group, which provided social and military functions and was the basis for same-gender sexuality. For some years the older warrior and younger male would pair off and become constant companions, intimates even in times of war. In general the younger boy would help to take care of the daily needs of his senior, which included looking after the camp, cutting firewood, cooking, and running errands, in addition to serving as sexual consort. Sex consisted of the older man coming between the legs of the younger boy, who is reported to have felt pleasure in the friction of his genitals rubbing against the older man. It was a special honor for the younger boy to carry the war shield of his partner when they traveled the country. It was expected that in time the older male would marry and the younger male, now grown up, would take a boy of his own. Even though this practice is now defunct, it stands as an important example of traditional homoerotic lifeways among males in Africa.

Homosexuality in colonial and contemporary Africa is more widely reported. Same-gender sexual practices among migrant older and younger male mine workers in South Africa provide an example of the circumstances in which these occur today (Moodie and Ndatshe 1994). Men from hinterland areas in South Africa who work in the gold mines often form sexual relationships with younger males. Under the old regime of apartheid in South Africa, such actions were punishable by severe penalties, but these probably added fuel to the terrible racism experienced before Nelson Mandela came to power and real tolerance was permitted (Gevisser and Cameron 1995). Boys in the mines did household chores, such as cooking, and joined the men in bed at night, serving as their "wives" or sexual partners for considerable periods of time. We can never know what the Azande warriors might have felt about their homoerotic partnerships, for they are long gone, but among contemporary mine workers the South African age-structured relationship resembles the Azande custom. It appears that the South African men enact their masculine roles as "husbands" and the boys serve as their "wives," suggesting that homoerotic bonds actually enable the older men to fulfill their expected gender roles in the absence of women. But in the case of the mine workers, the older men actually tell how they truly prize the boys and feel warm attachments to them, as the following statement by one of the men reveals: "We left the boys in the compound when we went to town, but we never spent the night in the township. We just spent a few hours with our girlfriends and then we returned to our boys. We loved them better" (Moodie and Ndatshe 1994, 134).

Cultural History of Homosexuality

Cultures vary enormously in social tolerance and acceptance of variations in human conduct, as expressed in their acceptance or rejection of other lifeways. Some cultures are paranoid, xenophobic, and aggressive; others are neutral or benign but unwilling to extend their basic rights to include the diverse lifeways of other cultures (Benedict 1934). The most progressive cultures are at the vanguard not only of tolerating but also of actually celebrating the range and diversity of cultural being. Sexuality and gender are perhaps the most critical of all political indicators of social tolerance for other ways of life.

A body of new scholarship divides homosexuality into distinctive cultural-historical forms of sexual desires and identities and the social relations that mesh with them. The concept of homosexuality itself—when viewed as a cultural idea shared in the group—must be placed in a historical framework of ideas that have emerged since the early modern period in western European and North American societies of European origin. In general, contrasts between heterosexual and homosexual and among normal, abnormal, masculine, and feminine have been widely regarded as essential, natural, and normal in the modern period of western history. But this was not always so.

Research in the anthropology and history of sexuality has demonstrated that the homosexual/heterosexual dichotomy as understood today in the western tradition is a product of the transition to modernity, although the exact causes and reasons are unclear. This sexual transformation involved such factors as the institutionalization of bourgeois middle-class values, the secularization of social medicine and state discourse on sexuality, the individualized concept of desire and identity, and the premium placed on reproduction within the nuclear family.

Homosexuality as a unitary construct derives from the Greek term *homos*, or "same," and not from the Latin *homo*, or "man," suggesting that the term historically referred to sexual relations between men or between women as persons of the same gender. In practice, however, a critical distinction has been made since the late nineteenth century between "homosexuality" as sociosexual contact between male partners and "lesbianism" as the form of sexual contact between females, with the male form the frequent cultural stereotype. This typology was preceded by other terms, most notably the *molly* in England, the *sodomite* (male) and the *sapphist* (female) in the eighteenth century more widely (Trumbach 1994), the *mannish lesbian* so feared in the later nineteenth and early twentieth centuries

(Smith-Rosenberg 1985), and *Uranian, invert,* and *intermediate sex* (Foucault 1980). The term *bisexuality* also made its debut in this time, conflating four different levels of meanings: biological, psychological, cultural, and behavioral (Herdt and Boxer 1995).

In the twentieth century, urban centers spawned a huge range of customs and names, from fairy to queer, as George Chauncey Jr. (1994) reports for New York. In the early part of the century, fairies could easily "put on" or "take off" mannerisms, including effeminate behaviors, much as they could change their clothes. But this should not be mistaken for a desire to change one's sex. As Stephen Murray (1996, 151) has remarked in this context, "Wanting to attract a man is not the same as wanting to be a woman." Today, although homosexuality refers to a wide spectrum of categorical identities, sometimes including some of the preceding terms but more commonly covering the gay/lesbian terminology now widely circulated, we should be careful not to confuse these terms with such antiquated notions as "pervert," "pedophile," "androgyny," "transsexual," or "transvestite," all of which occur in clinical medical and social science writings but designate different phenomena that lead away from the cultural forms of same-gender relationships described in this book.

Distinctions among these forms of same-gender contact rely on another contrast deriving from the clinical-medical or sexology tradition: sex and gender. This mid-twentieth-century distinction, as defined from the psychiatry and psychoanalytical writings of scholars John Money and Robert Stoller, respectively, stipulates "sex" for biological elements (e.g., genes, gonads, reproductive tracts) and "gender" for culturally learned and patterned roles, tasks, and identities (femininity and masculinity). A variety of critical analyses of this dualistic structure have typically been concerned with biological drives of an ahistorical or asocial nature and with the culturally ambiguous contrast between biology and culture or nature and culture (Vance 1991). Historically, distinctions between sex/sexuality and eros/body were rare and seldom explicit, being contingent on what people actually did in social relations from the time of the ancient Greeks to the turn of the century. By contrast, the concept of gender is typically regarded as a twentieth-century construction, though it was preceded by many distinctions that led to its study (Martin 1987). In the writings of Freud, for instance, gender does not occur as a marked concept, and sexuality and personality subsume the idea of socially patterned gender-specific roles or identities distinctive of femininity or masculinity as such. Homosexuality grossly incorporated aspects of all these.

Homosexuality in the last century was thought to reverse or "invert" gender. A man trapped in a woman's body, or a woman in a man's, was a common construction of the period. Some writers, such as Havelock Ellis, thought that male homosexuality was congenital and harmless and therefore excused the condition. Some, such as Freud, called the male homosexual a "psychic hermaphrodite." Today we would say that Freud viewed the homosexual as a kind of third sex, or what sexual reformers such as Edward Carpenter in England called an intermediate sex (Herdt 1994). But Ellis, being too committed to Darwinian ideas of reproduction, took a dark view of lesbians and was never willing to promote their cause. Indeed, he felt they should be treated as diseased or criminal outlaws (Smith-Rosenberg 1985). All such ideas are now passé and reveal more of gender and sexual stereotypes and attempts to socially control women and preserve the power of patriarchy than anything else.

The concept homosexual was coined about 1869 by German medical doctor Karl Ulrichs. He wrote a series of books in which he tried to show the "natural" variety of biological types of people who desired the same gender. Like many writers of his day, Ulrichs (and later Freud) leaned heavily on distinctions of "passive" and "active" as biological synonyms for "masculine" and "feminine." It was widely believed by homosexuals at the time that they were attracted only to "heterosexuals" and never to "inverts" like themselves. They apparently accepted uncritically the cultural stereotype that a male homosexual was like a "woman" and could be attracted only to a manly heterosexual. Gert Hekma (1994), a Dutch historical sociologist of sexuality, likes to refer to this kind of cultural idea as "border crossing" between homosexuals and heterosexual men in the last century. These stereotypes show the kinds of barriers the culture created to the possibilities of mutualistic or egalitarian relations that did not require dichotomous gender roles (man/woman) to be played out in bed. It was not until the early 1890s that the concept heterosexual, terminology that some attribute to British sexologist Havelock Ellis, entered popular discourse (Smith-Rosenberg 1985). Here again the ideology suggested that the man was attracted to the woman because she was different, passive, feminine, emotional—the list of paired oppositions and stereotypes made it difficult to achieve mutualistic relationships of equality between the genders too.

In the language of nineteenth-century sexual culture, the notion of homosexuality is believed to have come first because it pointed to what was atypical or was considered "abnormal" and "unnatural" (Weeks 1985). Thus, in the sexual ideology of the time degeneracy from heterosexual into homosexual was indicative of decay and disease, and these were signs to watch for in children and adults. Masturbation in particular was thought to lead to homosexuality and was the object of extreme control from the Jacksonian period onward in the United States. Whatever the case, the sexual dualism of male/female and homosexual/heterosexual created fundamental conflicts and oppositions in British and American societies. The heterosexual/homosexual dichotomy remains essential to the science and culture of our times even today.

When we say that homosexuality has been regarded as a disease since the last century, what do we mean? A whole theory of the degeneracy of normal into abnormal sexuality began to appear in medical and public health discussions in the last century. There was, for example, the peculiar idea that male homosexuals had female anuses, which drove them to desire penetration by other males as a manifestation of their disease. The idea that a homosexual man had a female brain, or a lesbian woman a male brain, was commonly believed to be the product of forces that had resulted in a degeneration of the capacity to attract the opposite sex, marry, and have children. Such a dichotomy of two sexes followed an earlier, more vague, and inclusive model that some scholars have referred to as a one-sex system, with the female form incorporated in the male body, somewhat in the manner of the biblical story of Eve's creation from Adam's rib. The point is that the female was regarded in medical, philosophical, and religious texts as an inferior form of the male body (Laqueur

1990). In very general and vague ways the link between this patriarchal ideology and the treatment of "effeminate" homosexuality as a disease suggests the tremendous threat that males loving males must have posed to men in the last century.

Masturbation was an ugly culprit in this game of shadows and accusations of decay and chaos in the body and society. Widely regarded as one of the primary diseases of degeneration, masturbation was routinely reported by doctors to be a leading cause of homosexuality and a variety of forms of mental illness, not to mention blindness, in the last century. Right into the 1930s children had devices placed on their bodies and in bed with them to prevent the slightest possibility of "self-abuse." Why were people so obsessed with masturbation? One reason may be that they regarded it as a dangerous degeneration leading away from marriage and the healthy reproductive desire to have sex with the other gender. Even Jean-Jacques Rousseau, so enlightened in many areas, nonetheless argues in his famous book *Emile* that masturbation is a social wrong, for some degenerates might wish to substitute the vice for marriage. Remember that in the spirit of the age, marriage was thought to be a key to how the social contract held society together—and this, according to Rousseau, superseded all other concerns in society.

Another important trait of the obsession with masturbation was the belief that it could be spread like a contagious disease. Even doctors subscribed to this "germ theory" of sexual degeneracy, in which they commonly advised parents to take care lest their children "catch" masturbation as they could measles or the common cold. Parents were advised to isolate the culprit children lest they spread the dirty practice. All kind of contraptions were designed to constrain the hands and movements of children, especially in bed at night, so as to prevent them from touching their own bodies. Since it was believed that masturbation could lead to diseases of the mind and body, then it followed that masturbation might bring on homosexuality, not to mention prostitution and other so-called unnatural practices. It is an indication of how much cultural standards can change through time and space that today these strange ideas and practices of sexual control seem more "unnatural" than the behavior the authorities sought to stop.

However, the description of masturbation being spread like a disease differs only slightly from cultural stories and media reports of how homosexuality can be "spread" by interaction with gays and lesbians. It is still common to hear reports of teachers who are removed from their positions because the fact that they are gay or lesbian has been discovered. The moralistic attitude underlying this discrimination seems to be that the teacher is like a parent and can influence the sexual ideas and values of the child in the direction of homosexuality. Indeed, the concept of in loco parentis, to substitute for the parent, is a guiding principle of education. But there is no evidence to suggest that an adult or another child can "teach" sexual desires, and even though sexual seduction and other means of sexual abuse occur in the schools as in other areas of society, the evidence does not suggest that teachers or gay and lesbian adults are perpetrators of abuse in this way. Rather, the notion that an individual can avoid becoming homosexual by avoiding homosexuals is the path of the pariah and testifies to the powerful barriers that exist within historical western culture to the acceptance of lesbians and gay men.

How much did medical science and ideas about sexual disease influence or create homosexuality as a category of western culture? The answer seems to be that medical science has been an immense influence on beliefs and ideas but that the presence of notions about same-gender desire are older than the medical theory. References to same-gender sexual relations more broadly can be traced in the western tradition to ancient societies, including Homeric Greece and the Roman Empire, and to the Middle Ages and the last part of the premodern period (before the sixteenth century).

The great French scholar of historical ideas Michel Foucault (himself a closet homosexual) is generally credited with the view that homosexuality began as a category in nineteenth-century social constructions of western European medicine and political economy. The rise of the medical clinic and the pursuit of medical knowledge created an alliance between the state and authorities that medicalized all categories of sexuality and gender and helped to better control people. Foucault (1980, 43) suggests that homosexuality was medicalized through a variety of practices that changed "the practice of sodomy onto a kind of interior androgyny, a hermaphroditism," a cultural idea that confused traits of the mind with those of the anatomy. Foucault (1980, 43) continues: "The sodomite had been a temporary aberration; the homosexual was now a species." In short, medical frameworks created mechanisms of social control and manipulations of power types of persons, including the cultural types homosexual/heterosexual.

Some historians now question this view and believe that Foucault failed to consider evidence from earlier periods that suggested that local ideas of same gender already existed before the birth of the clinic in the last century. What was labeled "homosexuality" as a marked category of disease and personology had already been anticipated by early modern period sources: folk psychology and medicine, then public health policy discourses, and later scientific sexology as the science of diseases of sexual "normality." Historians of the early modern period, including Randolph Trumbach (1994) on England and Theo van der Meer (1994) on Holland, date the emergence of the "sodomite" role (from sodomy, meaning unnatural intercourse, defined as nonreproductive sexual behavior) from the seventeenth century—well before Foucault and other scholars have suggested. Van der Meer describes letters and diaries of men who report how they desired the same gender and could not understand how they could have such feelings. Some Dutch men in the early 1700s reported feelings of intense desire and love for other men that are so remarkably modern in their flavor that they could be published as examples of love letters today. And yet the men could not see how they could have these feelings and felt that they were not "natural." These may be among the earliest known examples we have from western culture in which love and sexual preference for the same gender occur. It is remarkable that these intimate feelings and desires occurred more than a century before the concept of homosexuality was invented in Germany and quickly gained use throughout Europe.

According to the eighteenth-century worldview, all persons were capable of desiring both genders, at least on occasion; men could want smooth-skinned boys and women, lovely girls, and this did not necessarily violate their gender code. So long as genital penetration did not occur, these same-gender sexual relations and roles largely reinforced the patriarchy of the day. Yet the sodomites were classified as hermaphrodites; the women later classified as sapphists were physically examined for large clitorises, a sign of hermaphroditism. In fact, it has been argued that four genders emerged at this time: man, woman, sodomite, and sapphist. The sapphist was especially difficult for people to accept since the idea of a woman being manly, of passing as a man, of gaining male power and privilege through this means, was obviously a source of conflict and resistance to male authority and the control of female sexuality in the society of the times. Sodomy thus served as a new and emergent category of same-sex desire and practice in a variety of societies in western Europe. Such historiography suggests that distinctions in local culture and folk psychology were already relevant to discourses regarding the body, gender, eros, and same-sex desires that would lead to "homosexuality" a century before this was stipulated by Foucault's treatise.

These historical ideas of homosexuality and heterosexuality and hermaphroditism raise two general questions: Is a two-sex system composed of a biological male and a female universal? Is it possible that other cultures provide for a third sex or even multiple gender systems? The brief answer to both questions is yes. It has taken a very long time for westerners to understand such radically divergent sex/gender systems, largely because of their ethnocentrism and sexual chauvinism in judging other cultures against the standard of their own powerful sexual dimorphism idea (Herdt 1994). Some have argued, contra Charles Darwin, that a two-sex or two-gender system of classification and roles is the "natural and universal" way of being human, while others, such as Foucault, have suggested that this is an idea of the modern period in western culture. In either case it remains for us to ask whether westerners have exported their own system to foreign shores, imposing it on other cultures that were colonized and thereby changed, only later to see the same system reflected back in their own eyes.

A valuable lesson about third-sex systems can be drawn from the study of a rare form of hermaphroditism that may result in people being assigned at birth to the wrong sex. The condition is known to medicine as "5-alpha reductase deficiency," and it produces an unusual form of the hermaphrodite. These hermaphrodites, although genetically normal, are biologically different because of the failure of an enzyme to activate sexual differentiation at the tissue level in their bodies in the womb before they are born. At birth, then, they are born without normal-looking male genitals since the virilization of the appropriate areas on their bodies did not occur, and they may be mistaken for females. However, during puberty they undergo a second process of anatomical differentiation or virilization of their genitals because the sex hormone responsible for doing this is present to a certain extent in their blood. They may then begin to have a phallus that looks increasingly like a man's and less like a clitoris, with the result that society now has a manlike "woman" on its hands, which causes problems of all kind. The condition has now been reported from approximately a dozen countries around the world (I have studied it among the Sambia of New Guinea [1994]). What is remarkable about this condition is that it has existed long enough in some cultures, with enough individuals who are known to be anatomically different, that it is associated with the historical emergence of a third-sex category in these cultures. At birth, the person is thus socialized into the gender identity of being either male, female, or a third sex, and the culture provides customs and roles in the direction of the appropriate developmental line.

Individuals who grow up in this way typically think of themselves in the socially assigned category of gender role, either male, female, or hermaphroditic, no matter what their biological constitution. In cultures such as the Sambia, the society has long recognized the situation and has created three sex categories for sex assignment of the infant. In the third category—hermaphroditic—what is being marked is known as *kwolu-aatmwol*, or "turning into a man." Thus, the mistaken sex assignment should be understood as a transformation from female to third sex or hermaphrodite, not to male, as previously reported by the doctors (Herdt 1994).

Does biology or does culture rule in the development of gender identity? This was the question posed by a prior 5-alpha reductase study in the Dominican Republic when a group of American medical doctors suggested that hermaphrodites who were first identified as "women" later changed at puberty into "men," a condition that was known in the local culture as "penis at [age] twelve" (*guevedoche*).

This sexual transformation, the doctors believed, was caused by prenatal hormones that determine gender identity in the womb. Though culturally assigned to the female role, at puberty, the medical doctors suggested, these individuals had switched roles in the sex and gender system.

But the doctors ignored the existence of the local third-sex category, *guevedoche*. They thought of this as a sign not of a positive sex assignment and socialization in the culture but of abnormality and a failure of biology. In virtually all of the known cases they report, however, and in the other countries in which the condition has been made into a cultural category of sex assignment at birth, the evidence suggests that the sex of rearing outweighs the biological sex in the development of a gender identity and social identity. Biology is very important; but in human development, biology is part of a larger and more powerful process: cultural adaptation.

In studying the Sambia, I found that 5-alpha reductase hermaphrodites had long been known to exist and could typically be picked out by midwives at birth. Sometimes, however, they overlooked the child if its genitals strongly resembled a vulva and clitoris. Such a child would be reared as a female. But the others who were reared as *kwolu-aatmwol*, while socialized in the direction of maleness and masculinity, were never treated in the same way as other boys and men, as most profoundly expressed in the unwillingness of the culture to see the hermaphrodites through the whole process of male initiation into adulthood. Some of these individuals nevertheless became war leaders and renowned shamans, and one of them, Saku-lambei, has been studied by me over many years (Herdt and Stoller 1990).

The ones reared as women, however, were always socially pressured to convert from the female role to the third sex once they were discovered (around the time of marriage, when they could no longer hide their male genitals). They did not voluntarily choose exposure, but once it occurred, they made a practical decision under pressure to change social roles, motivated in part by the attractions of the greater privileges and power of being a "man." Of course, they were not "men" in the eyes of the Sambia; they moved to distant towns where they could pass as men and assume that social status.

The lesson from this study is of great general historical importance in debunking the myth of homosexuality, especially the perceived role of biology in determining gender identity. We need to be sensitive to the categories and cultural identities of other societies. It was the western medical doctors who had problems accepting the existence of third-sex categories in the local community. The local people had no trouble sorting each other out. When westerners have imported their own system of classification of sex and gender, the typical result has been contradictions and misinterpretations of these kinds.

This history of homosexuality in western culture and third-sex systems in western and nonwestern cultures shows that same-gender desires are susceptible to social influences. Previously, nineteenth-century ideas interpreted "sex" as meaning only reproduction and "natural" (missionary-position) opposite-sex intercourse. Other forms of sexual intercourse were therefore regarded as unnatural or abnormal, even though nonreproductive sexual behaviors may have been more frequent in the general population. All of these sexual attitudes show the bias and dualism that we have inherited from the Victorian worldview: male/female, heterosexual/homosexual, masculine/feminine, and, we now might add, nature/culture, or biology/society. What defies classification as male or female is thus by default unnatural. That is what the queer theorists poke fun at—the process that leads to the assumption of heterosexualism in all manner of things, even the behavior of lizards and spiders and seagulls, referred to in some texts as "homosexual lizards" and "heterosexual seagulls"! Therefore, sodomy—male/male sexual practice—is considered unnatural practice because it destroys the dualism in things and invites a kind of decay and chaos in the order of things.

It is easy to understand how such a powerful process of dualities can create images of duality in the cultural imagination of people. There are many "Dr. Jekyll and Mr. Hyde" stories during this period of the nineteenth century: of good doctors and evil counterparts, born of the imagery of public and secret, human and animal, with the good represented by the heterosexual or heteronormal bourgeois life and the evil by a second (split) personality haunting prostitutes and homosexuals and engaging in crime. The closet homosexual during the nineteenth century is a creature of hiding and of the dark spaces of society, a vampirish thing that haunts the margins of society to do nefarious deeds. The transformation from closet homosexual to late-twentieth-century gay and lesbian was tortuous but steady in civil progress. Because the gay movement had not yet exposed homophobia as a social and moral force suppressing people, homosexuality remained a problem of personal sin, disease, or psychopathology. The distinction between public-heterosexual and secret-homosexual continues to be prominent even today. But in time it was undercut by the enormous influence of the political movement of gay and lesbian reform, of liberation, and of the processes of coming out that have further complicated the dualism of public/secret. In the enormously controversial sexual reform and sexual liberation movements since that time, power—both social and political—has been at stake and has constantly been contested as gays and lesbians have fought to move from the margin to the center of society (Murray 1996).

Beginning in the last century and continuing well into the mid-twentieth century, strong preconceptions about the evils of homosexuality went without challenge. The "good and bad" rhetoric of the medical heterosexual/homosexual duality created moralism in secular affairs, while its underpinnings of sin and evil created intense sexual/political moralism in ultimate concerns about the soul after life, according to traditional Judaic and Christian religions. This moralism included the idea that same-gender sexual relations are sinful and satanic, an attitude only a small remove from the charge of witchcraft in the Inquisition of earlier centuries. The moralists always regarded same-gender sexual relations as deviant or perverse, as the biological product of a degeneracy of the "nerves," the vital fluids, the hormones, or the brain. When same-gender sexual relations were found in another civilization or society, the discovery either eroded all western confidence in the ethical standards of the civilization (Greek age-structured homoerotic relations perplexed people of the nineteenth century) or caused westerners to regard the other society as "savage" or "degenerate" (such attitudes can be found in colonists' descriptions of their first impressions of the New World, feudal Japan, and Old China, among other places). This sexual chauvinism is not gone from our present worldview.

The great sexual emancipation movements, beginning with the one in Germany in 1897, must be seen as responses to this marginalization and the abuse of rights of gay and lesbian people wherever these ideas were carried. Dr. Magnus Hirschfeld, the German medical doctor, thinker, and political and sexual reformer who led this movement, was inspired to teach and research the basic humanity of being homosexual in a time when the notion of homosexual as evil had begun to give way to its conception as a disease. The success of the homophile movement's attempt to persuade public opinion can be seen in the fact that not long after the turn of the century, the German parliament came close to actually passing a law to decriminalize homosexuality.

Ironically, by proposing that a biological difference made homosexuality a necessary condition to accept, the German homophile movement played into a tragic process. A reaction followed, and an alarm was sounded among right-wing extremists, particularly the Nazis. During these years, Hirschfeld and others continued to work for progress and appease the Nazis, who set about promoting heterosexualism, nationalism, and hatred of homosexuals and communists. Hirschfeld's efforts failed. What had begun as a moment of great promise ended thirty years later, in the late 1920s, when the Nazis attacked the Sex Institute in Berlin founded by Hirschfeld and burned it to the ground. Ultimately, the great doctor was forced to flee to France for his life, where he died broken and disappointed several years later. The Nazis, as we know, ultimately succeeded in taking over the government and systematically set about "cleansing" the Fatherland of Jews, homosexuals, and Gypsies, ending in the most terrible Holocaust in human history. We can never afford to forget the lessons of this horrible chapter in the manipulation of power in the name of nationalism and the misuse of biology and ideas of evil homosexuality to further it.

Many sexual reformers, humanists, and intellectuals have worked for social acceptance of homosexuals since that time, from Edward Carpenter in England, to Havelock Ellis and Freud in their own way, to modern feminists and writers such as Virginia Woolf and Gertrude Stein in a different way, on up to contemporary lesbians and gays who have worked for political causes. In one way or another these figures have challenged the fundamental idea that homosexuality is evil and abnormal, establishing either through medical, sociolegal, or literary texts the claim that same-gender desires and relationships are a part of the human condition.

Such a claim is very radical, even today. It started with nineteenth-century efforts to lobby for change in public attitudes, to gain acceptance of homosexuality as a medical condition that required compassion, not laws or prisons. Much was at stake, and many changed their minds. By expanding the concept of sexuality to include multiple desires for pleasure of all kinds, Freud implicitly moved to incorporate homosexuality into the range of normality in human life. However, he did so in steps and not without contradictions. He classified homosexuality as perversity in western culture in spite of remembering that the ancient Greeks had practiced age-structured homosexuality and mythologized the practice. Later Freud's view became more uniformly humane. Even in western society, Freud thought, sexual behavior was more diverse than was generally believed. In 1935 in a famous letter to an American mother, Freud advised her to accept and love her son in spite of his homosexuality. Since that time an avalanche of writing in medicine and psychology has humanized the many faces of homosexuality, enlarging on the point that creative and even gifted people have desired the same gender.

After World War II, Alfred Kinsey and his colleagues (1948), in a study of sexual behavior in American society, provided the first wide-scale statistical evidence to support the idea that homoerotic desires are part of life's spectrum. Homosexual behavior was more prevalent in American society than had been thought, Kinsey found, with 37 percent of American males experiencing same-gender sexual contact at some point in their lives. Although less than 5 percent of men and women enjoyed relatively permanent and lifelong adult sexual relationships with others of their same gender, this figure has been a political football ever since. The number 10 percent appeared later and was not the idea of Kinsey; perhaps it emerged from the subsequent political activism of gays or their critics (Michaels 1996). Kinsey himself never promoted this idea, but it has became established in the cultural imagination as a "magic number." In fact, the percentage of Americans who are more or less gay/lesbian identified is probably smaller since the best scientific survey study has found that only 3 percent of men and less than 2 percent of women are exclusively homosexual (Laumann et al. 1994). The critics have charged that these numbers are too low, and there is no doubt that certain people may be unwilling to report their sexual behavior even when research is done in such a careful manner. The actual numbers, however, are less important than the effect of Kinsey's work on American culture since he showed that sex for pleasure goes beyond reproduction and that the homosexual/heterosexual dichotomy is more of a cultural ideal than a fact.

Anthropologist Joseph Carrier (1980) has suggested that all cultures can be divided into ideal types of tolerance—approving, disapproving, or neutral with regard to homosexuality. We must be clear that any such cross-cultural study will always depend on the categories used and the sensitivity taken to local forms of same-gender relations. The Azande of Africa may allow for age-structured relations between boys and men, but the Azande penalize any other form of homosexuality that does not conform to this pattern. Should we categorize their culture as approving or as disapproving? The answer is neither. What matters are the ways in which each practice is created and represented and what political actions follow from conformity or resistance to the custom. A culture can have an emphasis on macho behavior and a cultural theme of machismo, or strident masculinity, in its institutions, but it can still allow for plenty of same-gender sexuality under certain conditions. Carrier's (1995) recent student of homosexuality in Mexico shows that same-gender sexual relations are rather common among males in the barrio. What matters is the type of sexual behavior that occurs. The dominant or insertive role for men is not stigmatized since a man is expected to be the inserter, and even though a man should marry and produce children and may prefer women to men, on occasion he may have discreet sexual relations with a passive male and still retain his honor and machismo. Mexico has also demonstrated change and growth in the development of a national gay and lesbian movement. Generally, Carrier has argued that the Euro–North American value system is more negative about same-gender sexual relations than other culture areas of the world.

In the United States negative attitudes about homosexuality actually worsened after World War II under the influence of the polarizing ideology of the Cold War. Homosexuality has ever since been a ideological football in a game of political rhetoric about "family values" and the role of the state in defining what is "natural and normal" (D'Emilio 1983). It became such a sinister and evil force in the eyes of conservative political demagogues, such as Senator Joseph McCarthy, that to be gay was to be hunted, resulting in the loss of jobs, friends and family, honor and dignity. McCarthy made it virtually impossible for anyone to conduct research on sexuality during this time. The secrecy of homosexuality necessarily intensified and made life painful for many. Ironically, of course, it resulted in new political activism among gays, support by heterosexuals who were tolerant, and the ultimate discrediting of McCarthyism as victimization. Nevertheless, the lives of many real homosexuals and others who were actually heterosexual but falsely accused of the "evil" were ruined or ended in the tragedy of suicide.

Soon, however, queers, homosexuals, and lesbians began to organize and fight back—joined by liberal heterosexuals, early feminists, beatniks, and other advocates of change. Among the first organized attempts to form a positive and protective association against homophobia was the creation of the Mattachine Society, a semisecret homophile movement of the 1950s, founded by such figures as the early activist Harry Hay. As Hay once remarked of this period and the perverse attacks on gays, the public understood the word *homosexual* to mean at the time what was perverse and defiant in "sick heterosexuals" who did unnatural criminal acts. It may be hard for us, looking back, to see to what extent the public refused to accept that people who seemed so "normal and natural" in every other respect, especially their gender roles, could be homosexual. This refusal was no doubt due to the strength of the inversion stereotype left over from the nineteenth century—a magical belief so powerful that many gays and lesbians had learned it and made the belief a part of their own self-concepts.

The intense political victimization and colonization of the self of the homosexual eventually led to the first scientific effort in the United States to actually measure the "normality" of homosexuality.

Well-known American psychologist Evelyn Hooker conducted interviews with closet homosexuals in the 1950s and 1960s to uncover a different reality. Some of these people were prominent and famous; many were successful and creative; all of them were closeted. The main finding of her study was that psychological tests of homosexuals appeared "normal" according to the personality measures of the times. Indeed, they looked so much like those of heterosexuals that experts who screened the tests without knowing who the subjects were could not pick out the homosexuals from the heterosexuals. This finding so startled many doctors and psychologists that they asked to see the research or tried to disprove it. Hooker was able to demonstrate that most stereotypes of the times had no basis in mental health concepts or psychological development. Indeed, she went on in the 1960s to demonstrate that the negative view of homosexual mental health was a product of society and homophobia. Generally, her closet homosexual friends in the 1950s, such as Christopher Isherwood, lived in two worlds—one public and one secret. They spent their leisure time in the company of friends, often in hidden bars or clubs, and constantly feared harassment and arrest by the police and exposure and blackmail. At work and in public these homosexuals had to hide their sexual identities and "pass" as straight. As I have shown from a historical sketch of the Chicago homosexual community during the 1960s, this kind of intensely fearful environment was widespread (Herdt and Boxer 1996). So terrible was the police manipulation in Chicago that gays routinely read the Sunday newspapers for the latest round of names of homosexual people arrested, certain that more lives were being exposed or ruined in the process. The anger that had begun after the McCarthy era continued to build and coalesced into political action. In this sexual culture the secret homosexual bars and clubs had their own ritual functions by providing for the induction of the closet homosexual into the lifeways of American homosexuality and by training and integrating the hidden into an emerging sexual minority.

We begin to see the key distinction that had emerged by the mid-1960s: that between those who were hidden and those who dared to be out. As Hooker showed in her groundbreaking studies of gay men, homosexual bar life was a means for those males who desired men of sharing sexual strivings. Heterosexual life, by contrast, was organized around getting married and having children. Indeed, we might go so far as to generalize that for the generation that came of age before the mid-1960s, the major ritual for homosexuals was hiding and passing as straight, whereas the major ritual for heterosexuals was being married in a church wedding. In fact, however, these rituals actually masked much discontent in American society, including the events and manipulations that were to lead to the Black Power movement, the women's liberation movement, and the gay liberation movement. Since that time, feminism has redefined the goals of women in ways that are instructive for an understanding of the changing meaning of the gay and lesbian formation today (Stimpson 1996).

The declassification of homosexuality as a disease by the American Psychiatric Association in 1973 generally fueled the gay movement not only in the United States but also in other countries. Until 1970 all basic issues of same-gender attractions, roles, and relationships were classified as a disease under the general diagnosis of "homosexuality." It was about this time that the explicit concept of "homophobia"—the conscious and unconscious fear and hatred of homosexuality and lesbians/gays—was coined in social study. The concept marks a turning point not only in scientific attitudes about homosexual mental health but also in the increasing self-esteem of many gays and lesbians, as noted in mental health studies during and since that time. Generally, the stigma and prejudice inherent in antihomosexual activities, such as queer-bashing, were implicitly accepted by society and sanctioned through the disease label. In many ways they still are (Herek 1993).

Medicine and psychiatry, however, continued to hold extremely negative attitudes until the gay and lesbian movement gained enough power to create a national and international debate about the question of whether homosexuality was a "mental illness." The field of psychiatry was itself divided, with a few leading authorities, such as Dr. Judd Marmor, Dr. Evelyn Hooker, and Dr. Robert J. Stoller, protesting that homosexuality was not a mental illness and should be declassified as a disease, while many adherents of the traditional "disease" view continued to oppose and obstruct the change. Long afterward, American psychoanalysis continued to regard homosexuality as a disease or at least as a neurotic disturbance, in spite of Freud's advice and the more positive acceptance of homosexuality in European psychoanalysis. It remains a mystery why until very recently American psychoanalysis was so intensely negative and even homophobic. Gradually such negative attitudes are ending, thanks to the criticism of such eminent analysts as the late Robert J. Stoller (1985, 183), who would write of the pernicious practice, "Stop picking on homosexuals, whether patients or colleagues."

A profound change in attitudes is occurring across the western countries. Evidence from social study shows that people who came of age before World War II were socialized into a cultural worldview that held terrible stereotypes of homosexuality. These included images that were not only the product of folk tales but were also reinforced by newspaper accounts of the exposure and arrest of "dirty men" who frequented public toilets and bus depots and whose arrest was published, together with their names, resulting in jailing, loss of jobs, public humiliation, and shame to their families. Such stories were associated with intense negative emotions in many families. The earlier generation seemed preoccupied with popular media images of dangerous stereotypes: lesbians as man-hating vampires, gay men as serial killers, child molesters, or promiscuous compulsives looking for sex in public toilets—tragic comic book images that continue to litter the cultural imagination. But these images—confirmed by society, taught to children, and thus learned by gays and lesbians as well—were so filled with rage, fear, shame, guilt, and alienation from the ordinary lives of everyday people that they could not possibly stand for long in a liberal democracy that prides itself on civic justice. Nevertheless, the damage done to a generation was painful and has not yet healed. All of the horrors of the AIDS epidemic, at first blamed on gays, and later on other oppressed minorities, has been a dark reminder of this tragic and long history of homosexuality as evil.

Ironically, however, some observers feel that the AIDS epidemic has done as much as anything else to transform the gay and lesbian community—not only into an effective political movement but also into a positive social community, a sexual minority culture, with its own symbols and institutions (Levine, Gagnon, and Nardi 1997). The epidemic, this Holocaust of gays at the end of the twentieth century, has wrenched the heart of people and time and again taken the best and brightest of the community's members in a terrible viral infection. The media attention to AIDS has both complicated and necessitated sex education and dissemination of information to the public, just as it has polarized the sexual moralists. And the times are changing, as larger numbers of boys and girls are more able to declare openly their same-gender desires in high school and college. The public has become aware of the positive transformation that has occurred in society, making it possible for more gays and lesbians to live an open life amid supportive friends and loved ones, at least in the cities, with the prospect of finding a place in the center of the larger society.

Is Homosexuality Universal?

Can we conclude that same-gender desires and relationships are universal and occur in all cultures? If so, what explains their presence? Are the reasons biological or social or some combination of both? Why are Americans so concerned with these issues anyway? These questions lead to a general principle: The western encounter with variations in gender and sexual roles and identities has historically tended to reduce the variety of behaviors and identities to one of three kinds of negative interpretations: (1) genetic, hormonal, or some other form of innate aberrance in utero; (2) biological degeneration, usually attributed to disease or some intrinsic abnormality, such as excess sex hormones; or (3) one or another psychosocial factors, such as a defect in early socialization (too much mother, too little father) or a deterioration of traditional social roles resulting from colonization and culture change.

Why is the public so interested in the search for an "ultimate cause" of homosexuality? Although several factors are relevant, it may be that western culture in general and Americans in particular remain wedded to the nineteenth-century idea that reproduction is the sole and ultimate reason for sexuality. Without reproduction, it is thought, "something went wrong," and "someone is to blame for the wrong."

It is very difficult to argue that homosexuality is universal, and this is not a position that I support. Anthropologists have generally resisted theories that attempted to explain a single trait or a common characteristic in all times and places by reference to innate or natural factors in the body or mind. Culture, as the key adaptive trait of our species, suggests the ability to learn new behavior and success in adapting to a large range of ecosystems, with their necessary prerequisites. Ideas that suggest how biological forces transcend or override culture and the history of anthropology and sexuality are replete with appeals to evolutionary models and pseudo-evolutionary hypotheses that later turned out to be overblown or even false. Time and again the history of sexuality research has shown that claims have been made for universal causes of homosexuality that turned out to be false, either in theory, method, or data. For example, nineteenth-century thinking commonly explained racial differences in intelligence by means of biological differences based on theoretical evolutionary developments, and only later, following important studies in the 1920s, did scientists discover that environmental factors explained these differences better than any internal model. This form of biologism tends to reduce sexual desire to biology and culture to a mere residue or frill of evolution.

Typically, evolutionary theories tend to treat homosexuality as a biological quirk or aberration or, at best, as a hidden adaptive advantage for the families that produce a homosexual. The notion that universal sexual drives might organize human development and society, as Darwin hinted, is particularly problematic since it gives priority to heterosexuality and reproduction over current social roles or identities. We know, however, that the entire population is not needed to reproduce itself, nor would we want it to, for that would probably contribute to problems of overpopulation, particularly in developing nations. Yet the biology/society dichotomy collapses when we realize that individuals vary within the group, often as much as individuals across groups. Thus, any theory of homosexuality must explain sexual variations within the life histories of individuals and within and across societies. Reductionistic biological theories of homosexuality have been notoriously unsuccessful as explanations of human sexuality. Individual human beings, whatever their divergent desires or modes of being, must adapt to their group and fit in, which suggests that the interaction of individual development and cultural roles will always be the most salient perspective in any understanding of the totality of human sexuality.

This is where universal models of homosexuality should be critically examined for hidden assumptions. To understand the conditions of oppression or freedom in the organization of homosexuality is to deal with all of the problems of human life and the struggle for dignity and freedom: love and hate, stigma, fear, secrecy, friendship, envy and power, political domination, and family loyalty and betrayal. We realize that in the hidden areas of society people who are kept in silence or suppressed or who never come to understand their own desires without social pressure are difficult to explain in the larger social pattern. But to study these individuals is also to challenge our general cultural ideas and beliefs about individual freedom and desires. The ancient Greek is not a homosexual, the Azande warrior who takes a boy lover is not gay, and the Sambia of New Guinea are neither of these and do not identify with these identities. To "export" such ideas and place them on other cultures constitute a kind of old-fashioned colonialism. In later chapters we see how the traditional forms of same-gender relations in places such as Thailand have confronted these western identity systems. We may think that the removal of political barriers and cultural taboos will somehow automatically free someone to come out as gay or lesbian, but the issue is not as simple as that because some individuals have lives wrapped in tradition and family and marriage that do not easily give way.

But is this thing that we call lesbian or gay in western culture the same in all other cultures? Perhaps what we label as homosexual is located only in western history or civilization. Perhaps it is ethnocentric to believe that the words and categories or identities that we use apply, or should apply, to everyone in other times and places? What if the social experience of growing up in western society, of using these words and concepts, so changed our understanding of sexual and gender relationships that it would simply be wrong to attribute the same meanings to people growing up in totally different countries, civilizations, and thought and language worlds. Rather than asking whether homosexuality is universal, then, we might be wiser to ask if same-gender relations occur in all times and places, what the optimal conditions are for the expression of same-sex desire, and how cultures and historical periods influence and treat these roles and behavior when they do occur. Such a comparison requires a different set of concepts that enables us to move beyond the confines of western society and history into other cultures.

◄ 3 ►

Same-Gender Relations
in Nonwestern Cultures

ACROSS THE GREAT RANGE OF nonwestern societies, sexual variations are common, but institutional forms of same-gender sexual relationships are not. It may be true that same-gender desires occur in
certain individuals in all times and places, but the cultural institutionalization of homoerotic relations is not universal. Indeed, homoerotic relations reflect the flavor and meanings of the local community and its place in (historical) society. Cultural institutions that
organize same-sex relations occur only within certain ancient and
kinship-bound societies in certain culture areas of the world. To
achieve the cultural institutionalization of conventional same-gender
practices suggests that homoerotic desires and practices are made a
part of the approved sexual lifeway characteristic of the kinship and
social relations of the whole society. We cannot separate the social
study of gays and lesbians in these groups from the overall cultural
patterns of marriage, parenting, family, religion, politics, and other
significant institutions. By contrast, for too long there has been a
tendency in the social study of the United States and similar western
countries to ignore the cultural fabric and reduce the entirety of gay
and lesbian lives to "sex acts" or "homosexuality," without regard
to the social, spiritual, political, and other elements involved.

As the ethnographies discussed in this chapter make clear, same-
gender desires were organized in three distinctive ways in some pre-

literate or archaic communities and in the tradition-bound tribal cultures of New Guinea, Asia, and other places. These three forms—based on age, gender transformations, and specialized social roles or practices—were as culturally elaborated as homosexuality in the modern period or egalitarian gay and lesbian roles in our time. Nevertheless, there were departures from customary practices as some of these societies began to modernize. But just as homosexuality cannot be said to be universal or biologically instinctual, so, too, we must not imagine some kind of linear evolution that leads from one type of social organization of same-gender desires to another type. All kind of social practices can be combined, borrowed, appropriated, recombined, rejected, and ultimately made over into an image that has the same appearance as another but is actually a different experiential and symbolic form. That is the genius of culture.

Age-Structured Homoerotic Relationships

Cultural and social systems that organize homoerotic encounters and relationships between the genders according to age distinctions are a powerful means for understanding comparative forms of homosexuality in ancient and modern times. Although some authorities, such as Ford and Beach (1951), have claimed that gender transformation outweighs age in the social organization of homoeroticism, I am skeptical of this claim, for reasons that become apparent throughout this chapter. Even when gender transformation dominates social organization, age distinctions are still of importance in how gender is expressed in local relationships and in parallel systems of age-grading that exist alongside the gendered form.

But age-graded forms of homoerotic relations are clearly more frequent among males than among females around the world. Typically, age-structured relations are between males—younger boys and older adolescents or young men. These relationships provide the basis for status differences between persons that may continue throughout the life cycle into old age, even on the level of the grandfather's generation. Societies with age-graded same-gender relations provided for these customs in several ways. They utilized rituals, gender segregation, kinship rules and taboos, arranged marriages, and marked sexual dichotomies between men and women. In general, these cultures regarded age and generation as important markers of cultural knowledge, power, wealth, and wisdom in men and women. As agrarian societies, they were also enmeshed in religion and ritual initiation not only to create proper moral and spiritual development in the younger child, but sometimes also to teach beliefs about how to physically "grow" or attain competence. Furthermore, education or pedagogy and social advancement were at times linked to initiation in cults of age-graded homoerotic relations. In some cases, like those of the New Guinea Sambia, and probably those of the Azande, boys were thought to require ritual treatment to masculinize their bodies and minds, making them into proud, honorable, strong warrior-citizens and manly, marriageable partners who would defend the community and father children to carry on the tradition of family and village. In short, there was no antagonism between same-gender relations and the development of masculinity and male honor since boys were expected to later marry and father children. So long as these social requirements were met, and the honor of the boy was maintained, a boy and a man's relationship fulfilled the standards of the society and was prized.

Homoerotic relations established by age norms and age-graded cohort or generational practices are among the most ancient and pervasive of all homoerotic relationships in the world. The ages may vary across cultures, with the youngest being in middle childhood (aged seven and older), and the oldest continuing into late adolescence or early adulthood (the physical ages of which vary according to how late puberty comes on, which in New Guinea could be around age fifteen and in the ancient civilizations could be perhaps a bit older). Among the Sambia of Papua New Guinea, for example, age-structured relations commence between the ages of seven to ten years of age for boys, who undergo collective ritual initiations into a secret men's society that prescribes and supports these practices for many years (Herdt 1981). The roles may also vary according to the economy and social structure of the people, its ideas of power and its actual hierarchy, as noted in writings by such authors as myself

(1987b), Barry Adam (1986), David Greenberg (1988), and Stephen Murray (1992a).

Ancient Societies

In the great civilizations of the world, including the antique societies studied here, systems of sexual exchange and prestige relations based on age were common. Indeed, these were among the most significant of ancient societies, and they included notable age-structured same-gender relations in Homeric Greece, ancient China, Korea, and, later, feudal Japan. The vitality and honor of the men, as well as the education, prestige, masculine growth, and well-being of the partners, were constantly being promoted through a social economy of age-asymmetric sexual relations. This required marriage and fatherhood, on the one hand, and passionate and companionate relations with younger males, on the other. In early Homeric Greece a warrior's lifeway, his rough-and-ready masculinity, were inculcated through boy-inseminating practices. In the instance of Homeric Greece, a cultural transformation from a warrior complex into a philosophical one took on mythological proportions in later ages. An emphasis in these cultures on insemination and warrior life seems to have given way to cultural elaboration of sexual and gender relations more broadly. Age-structured relations found later in a variety of Indo-European traditions, including Teutonic tribes and those in the Balkan Mountains around present-day Albania, have been typically traced back to the classical/mythological homosexuality (in the opinion of scholars such as J. J. Winkler, Kenneth Dover, David Halperin, and Bernard Sergent, all reviewed in Herdt 1993). Premodern societies thus acknowledged the existence of intergenerational male relations—which did not feminize or dishonor the boy or violate the gendered position of the man—so long as no reversal of the active/passive dichotomy occurred between them.

Centuries later Renaissance poetry borrowed from classical sources mythic ideas about the love of boys. These ideas found their way into the sonnets of William Shakespeare, for example. Generally, Renaissance writers accepted the fact of romance and sexual desire for another male, especially the handsome youth admired in courtly societies (Smith 1991). Among the most powerful evidence for such cultural ideas in practice comes from medieval Italy, in which approximately one-third of all men were convicted of sodomy with boys (Rocke 1988). And even today the social justification of age-asymmetric homosexuality turns to the archaic traditions for its arguments.

Ancient Greece. Homoerotic relations between older and younger males, and to a lesser extent between older and younger females, were known in Greece and the Hellenistic world from at least 800 B.C. Among the ancient Dorians of Crete, the practice of boy love was created through a kind of symbolic "capture" of a desired boy by an older youth. They "eloped" in this way, and to acknowledge their sexual relationship, the family and community gave gifts and provided feasts. Eventually the males would marry, and the boy would in turn take a younger lover. Although we cannot be sure, such a practice may have been the historical basis for later ritual homoerotic practices among Greeks nearer to the time of Plato. The custom in symbolic form may also have been enacted in the myth of Zeus and Ganymede, among others: The god was so swept away by the beauty of the boy that Zeus abducted him. The theme of boy love and capture is repeated later in the story of Chrysippus, a beautiful boy who so charmed the older man Laius (the father of Oedipus). Mythologically, a chain of ruinous events follows, leading to the tragedy of Oedipus, who unwittingly killed his father and married his mother and eventually blinded himself to stop the Fates from doing more harm. The story suggests divine retribution for Laius's violation of Chrysippus and the destructive power of homosexuality in society. Not only does the story remind us of the many mythological linkages between warrior homoeroticism and masculinity, but it also signals the apocalyptic element in mythological homosexuality based on man/boy sexuality and love in classical times.

The structural relationship between the older and the younger male in ancient Greece was formalized by a code of honor and love. In such matters the concept of *areté* (male strength) was central. The Greek ideal of *areté*—of male virility, honor, courage, beauty, and nobility—was symbolized in the secular world by the athlete and warrior and in the heavenly world of the gods by the power and divine seed of the gods. But when imagining the material form of *areté,* the Greeks liked to compare the fire and energy of *areté* to the great strength of a stallion in the chase. Male lovers were known as *eromenos* (boy, beloved) and *erastes* (senior, lover); the age of the younger male could range from twelve to twenty, since the onset of puberty was much later than in our time, or until the appearance of a beard on his face. Most authorities believe that the sexual practice of these men was primarily or exclusively intracrural (between the legs), as in the case of the Azande; the younger male may not have experienced ejaculation. It is widely agreed that the honor of the boy had to be preserved at all costs and that his consent was required for all homoerotic relations.

We know that such relations in Homeric times were culturally concerned with the boy's physical strength and well-being, with his prowess and bravery, and with his entrance into the warrior traditions of honorable masculinity. Certainly, the Thebans and Spartans took boy lovers as comrades and bedmates. As these youths grew older, they learned all of the traits of the warrior and later took younger boys themselves. Here again we are reminded both of the Sambia of New Guinea and of the Azande of Africa. As the centuries passed, the physical emphasis was transformed into more of an educational and philosophical one, but the promotion into noble masculinity remained.

After the fall of ancient Greece, the link between same-gender noble homosexuality and warrior life was remarked by Greek authorities themselves and by the Romans who followed and admired them but were ambivalent about homosexuality, especially after the emperor Augustus. Since tribal societies in ancient Indo-European traditions, as well as elsewhere, practiced age-structured relationships along with warrior training, it is understandable that some writers have sought common origins or causes of homosexuality in gender segregation and warrior life. Certainly, these conditions were combined in ancient Sparta, where warriors lived separately from their wives. In the most famous of all such groups in the ancient world, known as the Sacred Band of Thebes, the erotic unions of male warrior couples were thought to have created a mythological and invincible courage. To quote Plutarch in the matter, "An army consisting of lovers and their beloved ones, fighting at each other's side, although a mere handful, would overcome the whole world" (cited in Westermark 1917, 479).

In the centuries leading up to the time of Socrates, the mentoring or pedagogical qualities of the man/boy relationship were emphasized. By the time of Plato, the erotic quality of the relationship was altered; the educational function replaced the warrior one in all but name. A philosophical and romantic pedagogy existed in which the older male helped to introduce the boy to social life and protected his honor on the stage of the Gymnasium and in political affairs at large as a citizen of the polis. We must be careful to realize that for the Greeks, these customs did not oppose marriage or fatherhood. Indeed, a Greek citizen could not achieve full personhood unless he married into the proper family and fathered children to carry on the family name and estate. In Greece and for the most part in the later Roman Empire, intracrural or anal sex could be described by a word roughly meaning "homoerotic," but the people who engaged in this practice could never be described as "homosexuals." Here, the emphasis was on doing rather than being, on a person's sociosexual relationship rather than on his inner sexual nature. Sexual relations and the particular acts of relations with boys were in accord with the gender roles of the times, and they did not stereotype men or place them in categories separate from other men. In short, sexual identity distinctions of homosexual and gay did not yet exist and would await their invention in the modern period. In fact, the concept of sexual identity divides the Greeks and all ancient societies East and West from our own concepts and concerns with classifications of people in sexual categories.

In general, homoerotic relations between adult free citizens were ridiculed and later disliked among the Greeks because such activities suggested the dishonor of slaves. Only unequal-aged homoerotic relations were approved, but only so long as they preserved the honor of the boy. Furthermore, a male was obliged to marry and produce children to further the family, clan, and estate. Whatever sexual relations existed in private, including sexual relations between a master and slave or with a prostitute, a different code of behavior applied. Sexual relations could include sex between these adults and might include homoerotic relations, though these were among social or class unequals and therefore did not violate the code of honor. Even here, however, the reputation of the higher-status man could be smeared by the revelation of these activities, and he took great pains to avoid such a potentially destabilizing affront to the Greek social hierarchy.

The Greek lifeway thus commanded a masculine code of sexual relations that generally made all partners, men and women, older and younger males, citizen and slave, of higher and lower social status. Not until we come to the modern period do we begin to see a notion of equality in sexual relations become an ideal. Especially vital were respect and honor for the boy, whose consent for homoerotic relations had to be gained through courting; in some cases the permission of his family had to be sought first. Honor had to be upheld at all costs, much in the same way that the good honor of a woman as a virgin had to be upheld until she was properly married or the honor of a married woman could not be smudged by accusations of adultery. In these ways concern was focused on the boy's desires and wishes for sexual and social relations with the older man. This dynamic probably prevailed in many of the relations known in ancient Greece, possibly more widely in ancient Celtic and Teutonic sexual practices, and in those spread into hinterland areas of Europe and the Mediterranean.

Ancient China, Korea, and Feudal Japan.   Traditional same-gender relations among older and younger men existed in China for a long time, perhaps as far back as the Bronze Age, but certainly by the time of the Zhou dynasty (1122–256 B.C.). A kind of elaborated sexual worldview accepted same-gender desires rather openly, including open admiration for men's beauty and public expression of desire for another man. Particularly among the elite and socially privileged classes, homoerotic relations between men and youths were enjoyed by many right up to the twentieth century, after which homoeroticism was considered a form of "moral degeneracy" and forbidden. Under the regimes of this century, homosexuality has generally been disapproved, if largely ignored, somehow the result of colonialism or anti-Chinese sentiment. Today Hong Kong newspapers suggest that China may implicitly promote homosexuality through the culture's preference for boy children and the government's control of reproduction. Historically, however, tolerance of homosexuality was a kind of divide between China and the West. Most of the historical reports are concerned with men. There is very little to be found about women's sexual relations and lesbianism in old China, though in the nineteenth century a special economic role and class of women silk workers in the Pearl River valley provided the historical basis for women/women homoerotic relations.

The poetry and folktales of China do not generally refer to same-gender desire as an innate essence but rather as a matter of what a person feels or desires and does. Once again the emphasis is on doing, not being. No concepts of sexual identity or of "the homosexual" per se are to be found in China. This tendency is in keeping with the view in nonwestern cultures, as we have seen, that people's sexuality is a result of kinship, marriage, and social roles and practices rather than of internal sexual drives or desires in any simple sense. Nevertheless, some notion of homoerotic desire as a permanent condition of certain individuals does seem to occur in Chinese literature. Indeed, the famed Ming dynasty novels of "Judge Dee," set down by the Dutch scholar Robert van Gulik, suggested that people who desired sexual relations with others of the same gender found strange pleasure in this part of their "nature." Anal intercourse was most common. Dominance and submission relations were typically structured by age, gender, and social status, which influenced the forms of sexuality. Yet these patterns transformed the individual across the life course, for just as a boy and an adolescent would take the passive sexual role with older men, so as adults they would take the active role with younger males. Exceptions to this pattern can be found in old stories, however. Chinese history shows that many men experienced both same-gender and other-gender relations during their lives, having marriage and children alongside younger male lovers.

Another Chinese practice of age-structured homoerotic relations took the form of fictive kinship between men in Fujian Province in southeastern China. This practice has been known since at least the seventeenth century, when a Dutch observer referred to men in the area as "filthy pederasts" (Hinsch 1990, 130). These relations were common in official circles. Among high court officials and the literati, and perhaps Confucian scholars and priests, unions were cultivated in which the older man was called "adoptive older brother" and the younger, "adoptive younger brother." The erotic relationship between the men apparently could go on for life. Here was an invocation of a form of fictive kinship and brother love that included sexual relations but was also characteristic of the times (Hinsch 1990, 131). An exceptionally strong friendship was ceremonialized through ritual sacrifice of fish, rooster, and duck and a swearing of everlasting mutual loyalty. This dedication created an enduring bond of age-structured loyalty, the older male always remaining the "elder" in their bonds of fraternal affection.

China is a vast, complex society, and other forms of same-gender relations have been recorded there, including gender-reversed behavior by men who played female/feminine roles. Moreover, the existence of castrates, of certain eunuchs who favored men over women, is also reported. Class barriers could also be broken down in the special same-gender friendships that combined sex in this period of China. Commercial sex between males was also present, typically featuring older and younger, richer and poorer males, in unions. Indeed, there is a vague sense in the Ming literature that permanent desire for sex with another male is not natural but is also not rare, and in general the sexual culture of the Ming dynasty accepted this as part of the design of things in nature and culture. Even a form of "egalitarian homosexuality" is known from the story of teenage male love recorded in the famous old Chinese novel *Dream of the Red Chamber*, the romantics of which suggest an undying love that we would today call homosexual (Hinsch 1990, 13). That erotic tale reminds us that the West had no monopoly on romance or same-gender ideals of love and companionate equality in times past.

Similar cultural patterns are known from ancient Korea, which shares a variety of historical features with China, once the occupier of the smaller country. Erotic attraction to boys was known and implemented in court society, among other areas. The customary role of the so-called flower boys (*hwarang*) of Silla is notable from the Yi dynasty in Korea (Herdt 1987a). Apparently the idea of *midong*, or "good-looking boys," commonly had homoerotic overtones in the discourse of older men. Especially beautiful boys might be taken into wandering folk operas and musical groups that toured the country. Here the boys could be dressed as girls to take parts in operas, plays, and songs, accompanied by musicians and minstrels. The boys were said on occasion to be "married" to the older performers and served as a sort of "wife" to the entertainers. A tradition of shamanism and healing is also related to these customs, though the literary and theatrical aspects of the age-structured and gender-transformed homoerotic roles of the boys seem especially significant. Here we have the first example of a traditional homoerotic practice that cannot be neatly packaged by functions of age or gender, and we should be careful not to impose rigid definitions and neat classifications on what were obviously rich and remarkably complicated sociosexual relations.

Homoerotic relations in feudal Japan are of particular interest to the cross-cultural study of same-gender relations because they bridge ancient and modern times. Interestingly enough, Japanese popular belief, a reflection of myth and legend, suggests that "homosexuality" (*nanshoku*) was introduced from China by the Buddhist monk Kukai centuries ago (Leupp 1996). Japan provides extraordinary cultural examples during the Edo period of age-structured relations that also involved gender change in samurai warriors and in court relations associated with the Kabuki theater. Moreover, traces of these traditions are still to be found in Japanese literature and symbolism regarding contemporary roles of gay/lesbian and homosexual today. Much new work is emerging on these important traditions (Pflugfelder 1992) in the Edo and Tokugawa periods of Japanese history.

Boy love seems to have been prominent in the Buddhist tradition, particularly among Japanese Buddhist monks. Early Buddhism in Japan created sexual lifeways that may have implicitly promoted homoerotic relations. These included the renunciation of the material world and sexual relations between men and women, gender segregation in the monastery, and forms of teaching and worship that implicitly idealized the love between teacher and student or neophyte. These relations had to do in part with the inferior position of women in the society and with the military nature of male social relations as well. As in ancient Greece, China, and elsewhere, marriage was a political and social arrangement, not a matter of intimacy and love. Men sought emotional closeness elsewhere, with boys, prostitutes, or other male intimates. Although in many of these traditions, including Buddhist monasteries in Thailand today, there was no requirement for same-gender sexual relations, neither was there a taboo against them, although the master/student relationship carried responsibilities and restrictions that complicated a homoerotic relationship when one developed. Furthermore, the great literary works that immortalized homosexuality were written by monks. The intimacy of the master/novice relationship certainly created the kind of social and psychological condition that might have fostered same-gender desire and eros. Even the famed aesthetics of the Japanese Zen Buddhist practice may have played a role in the creation of age-structured homosexuality. The beauty of the boy was regarded as perishable and impermanent—much like the short-lived cherry blossom famed in the art of Japan. Each year the blossoms came, but they were never quite the same, and they would eventually fade. Likewise, the blossom of a boy's body, once radiant, would wither. As Murray (1992a) has reported, the cultivation of the beauty and renown of boys was so well known that it remains memorialized in poetry and folktales up to this day.

Samurai, who were warriors of high status in feudal Japan, had sexual relations with younger males, including boys in training to become warriors, as a matter of course. Great shoguns and samurai kept boy lovers to provide both emotional and sexual pleasure. Culturally sanctioned attachments to younger male lovers, or *nenja,* were part of the noble tradition of the production of warrior masculinity that we have seen in prior examples. But in feudal Japan another dimension obtained: A man could gain prestige and prowess through courting (in which his performance was dominant) and through having numbers of male sexual partners. So long as the older or socially dominant male took the role of the "man" with his partner, no question about the man's honor or the masculinity of the youth would be raised. A *nenja* could be of the same age but not of the same social status as the other man.

Of course, not all Japanese men had such relations. Some of them disliked the love of boys intensely, preferring women to boys; while others disliked *nenja* but still took plenty of them as lovers. According to the etiquette of the time, the younger male was supposed to respond to the passions of the older one, no matter how ugly or unattractive the older man. What was emphasized was the selflessness of the young man in his sense of duty to alleviate suffering—in this case, the burning desire in the older man's being. Today we can find allusions to such sentiments in the homoerotic writings of the Japanese novelist Yukio Mishima, particularly as expressed in his masterpiece *Forbidden Colors*, in which the burning desires and painful rejections of love between older and younger men are a theme.

In relations with samurai, it does not seem that boys changed their appearance or acted feminine. But this was to change in the context of the Kabuki theater. After 1612 it became increasingly common for all the theater roles to be played by boys and men, though female impersonation was controversial and elaborate decrees attempted to control the situation, such as a code that dictated the proper length of hair among admired and beautiful youths. Thus, the feminine-looking male actors could become cross-gendered lovers of men, like transvestites. Indeed, legend tells that the Kabuki theater originated from a shogun's preference for seeing only male performers. The boys were dressed in colorful and lavish clothes and makeup, sometimes in the manner of exquisite girls. They were the object of male desire and display, of courtly intrigues and rivalries. The boys' long forelocks were said to be the real glory of their role, and later, when shearing of the hair of these boys was done for political reasons, it is said to have sparked "tears of blood" in the spectators (Murray 1992a, 121). Likewise, as we have seen in old Korea, age-structured relations combined with the theater tradition of beautiful boys dressing as women in the touring companies of performers—suggesting the traveling performances of Homeric bards in ancient Greece.

After the seventeenth century, some of the more powerful shoguns of the Tokugawa period were known to favor attractive youths and officially appointed them to the courts with the general expectation that they would become sexual partners. In *Comrade Loves of the Samurai*, by seventeenth-century Japanese novelist Saikaku Ihara, we find many romantic tales of how samurai sons were urged by their families to form homoerotic alliances with warriors that matured into lifelong companionships, right alongside marriages to women. The romantic idea was that the samurai might keep his favored male partner by his side in battle. Exceptional cases are reported in which two men stayed together for life, the younger one aging but continuing in the role of the "youth." Up to the time of the Meiji era (1868), relations between older and younger males were apparently common. But with the opening of Japan to western influence, the negative attitudes of Christianity and western sexual chauvinism seemed to take hold, intolerance toward homosexuality arose, and relationships with boys largely ended. Homoerotic relations remain highly structured in contemporary Japan, and homosexuality remains a controversial and often hidden issue.

African Societies

Little is known about homosexuality and same-gender relations in Africa and least of all in sub-Saharan Africa. Only a few scholars have had a serious interest in finding out whether, and if so in what ways, Africans have enjoyed sexual relations with others of the same gender. We do know that in certain countries the effort to understand these issues has often met with hostility. Moreover, colonial attitudes and laws left over from the French and British and other western powers definitely continue to influence certain African countries. As noted in Chapter 2, homosexuality is treated with contempt. Some researchers have nevertheless encountered several forms of pre- and postcolonial same-gender sexual behavior. Africa is, after all, a large continent, and contrary to what is said about a common "African culture," the diversity of its cultures and peoples is great. Hence, there are no uniform same-gender sexual customs, and we should take care in generalizing about them.

In North Africa age-structured same-gender relations are best known historically from the oasis village of Siiwa, in the Libyan desert, which is said to retain one of the oldest forms of Near Eastern sexual customs. Some even date this form to a mythic ancient

Greek tradition! Although the entire community converted to Islam in A.D. 1100, man/boy sexual relations existed until recent times. Siiwa also practiced widespread extramarital relations between women and men and public ritual sexual practice done on special ceremonial occasions (Gregerson 1994, 215–217). Boy marriage to an older male was known throughout the area. Boys between the ages of twelve and eighteen could be officially married to an older man or rented out for a night, and prominent men were said to lend their sons to each other for this reason. Love affairs and jealousies over the boys were common. English novelist Robin Maugham reported of the Siiwai: "They will kill each other for a boy. Never for a woman" (Gregerson 1994, 216).

It may be that these practices were cultural survivals from an earlier historical formation, possibly even a variant of Zoroastrianism, which came to dominate areas of the Middle East but in a pure form died out after the fifteenth century. Although age-structured homoerotic relationships are said to occur in other areas of North Africa, the documentation is poor, and it is unclear whether village practices such as that of Siiwa still survive.

Sub-Saharan societies are also known in which men had sex with men and women with women. One of the most famous examples in the anthropological literature describes the Azande people, who live in southern Sudan. Theirs is a complex and remarkable society. Anthropologist E. E. Evans-Pritchard described three conditions that led to age-structured sexual relations between men, which he observed in fieldwork.

First, some of the young Azande men lived at the court as soldiers. It was difficult for these soldiers to obtain a wife because they did not yet have the resources to pay the high bride price. The women, moreover, were often promised in marriage from the time of birth. Sexual taboos were strictly enforced. Thus, the only way in which the young bachelors could have relationships with women was in adulterous affairs. But this was extremely dangerous, for if the affair was discovered, the male offender could be punished with severe mutilation, even death. The young bachelors would therefore seek partnerships with younger males, sometimes even very young boys, with whom they would establish sexual intimacy and companionship. These relationships were socially accepted and as legitimate as marriages between husband and wife and were in fact referred to as "marriages" in the more or less open popular language and court discourse of the times. However, these partnerships were not expected to last forever; just as in the prior cases of the ancient Greeks and the Sambia of New Guinea, it was customary for homoerotic relationships to end after a certain number of years. Eventually both the older bachelors, and later the boys in turn, would marry women and rear families. We therefore have no reason to believe that Azande men preferred boys to women, and the system of control of women suggests the contrary. But what is important is that the Azande warriors experienced such relationships as a part of their life cycle and never seem to have felt at odds with this sexual lifeway.

This form of marriage between a young man and a boy disappeared after colonization by the British. Presumably, it became easier for the men to obtain a wife. Furthermore, the punishments for adultery were no longer as severe as before colonial rule. Evans-Pritchard does not confirm whether the British forbade same-sex relations altogether, although it is well known that they outlawed homosexuality in the countries they colonized.

Second, age-structured homoerotic relations grew out of special cultural taboos. The Azande practiced a kind of ritual soothsaying known as the "poison oracle." An ordeal by poison was believed to foretell the future, but the warrior had to be in a "sexually pure" condition to make the practice work. A man was tabooed from sleeping with a woman or having sex with her the night before he consulted the oracle, for the Azande believed that she would spoil the outcome. Boys would not spoil the oracle, and spending the night with them was perfectly acceptable, and perhaps even encouraged, for this reason. At any rate such a custom provided ready support to take a boy.

Third, the Azande princes at the royal court did not have anything to say about their future marriages partners or about the timing of their weddings. They were almost totally the pawns of political and kinship alliances. These princes, while waiting for their fathers to arrange their marriages, took in servants. The princes would be accompanied by these servants wherever they went, and these servants were a fixture of court society. They were kept for cooking, cleaning, and performing certain ceremonial and warrior duties in support of the men, and they were kept for sexual pleasure as well. The princes may have favored certain boys and advanced them over others in this way.

Azande custom thus led the boy partners to take on "wifely" routines and functions apparently modeled after the social and sexual roles of wives. These relations were always understood to be temporary. When the boy partner grew older, his former lover might help him in securing a wife. But the purpose of the marriages with boys was understood to be the pleasure of the older men. This difference in age is crucial in an understanding of the kinds of relationships that men and boys could practice among the Azande.

Azande women, in contrast, had relationships with other women on occasion, but in those cases age was not an important organizing principle. Formal homoerotic marriage arrangements did not exist. Sometimes two women who had the same husband developed a sexual relationship, perhaps enabled by the circumstance of being co-wives. But this was not a necessary condition for the development of sexual intimacy or a love affair between them. In fact, what we know about these relations suggests that all that was really necessary was for there to be affection between the two women. We know far less about relations between women than about those between men because Evans-Pritchard had fewer occasions and perhaps less interest in talking intimately with women than with men.

It is especially remarkable that such a customary intimacy was known among the Azande, given their marriage and warrior practices. We may never fully understand the historical reasons that led to these practices, but the existence of same-gender sexual relations among both men and women stands as a reason never to presume that we can predict what we will find in the full range of sexual variation across cultures.

In another contemporary southern African culture, Lesotho, age difference was important in relationships between young women who were attached and became homoerotically bonded. These are the "mummy-baby" relationships studied by anthropologist Judith Gay (1986). These romantic and sexual friendships seemed to model the kind of courting and, later, marital relations the women might find with men. The women referred to each other with the English terms *mummies* (older) and *babies* (younger), a form of fictive kinship that ensured social support and cultural validation of desires and affections.

Young women engaged in mummy/baby relations when they first entered adolescence. These distinctive bonds involved increasing degrees of intimacy, including open expressions of kissing, and might go on to the deepest sexual and lifelong bonds, though not so far that later marriage with a man was prevented. The roles of the older women were very different from those of the younger one, especially in terms of social obligations. The older woman took on the responsible role in the relationship, and she provided her younger partner with gifts and advice. The latter was important because it prepared the young girl for future relationships with men, most significantly her future husband. A woman might continue this relationship for some time after she was married. But then she would cease seeing her younger partner, who then in turn would find a younger woman of her own. The roles would change, and she would now be the one providing gifts and advice. Such relationships were consistent with Lesotho notions of growing up and maturing. They play an important part in preparing girls for all future sociosexual relationships, including heterosexual roles when they reached maturity. That the young women really loved each other and saw their relationship as an exchange of affection seems clear from the intense attachments reported. More than that, the Lesotho women enjoyed the romantic/sexual part of the relationship in its own right.

Whenever homosexuality and same-gender relations are mentioned in the African literature, they are invariably treated negatively, and the suggestion is always that they were imported from the outside. It is clear that this sexual chauvinism is a part of a reaction to colonialism and a projection of the Other onto the homosexual. In the history of the Azande, however, we see that the reverse was closer to the truth. If anything, the British colonizers tried to stop same-sex practices. Indeed, in many countries in Africa they forbade homosexuality by law. These laws are mostly in existence today. Only in South Africa, under the freedom of the new government that replaced the cruel oppression of apartheid, do we find the beginnings of the first gay and lesbian social movement in Africa, which is cause of great interest throughout the region (Gevisser and Cameron 1995).

New Guinea Societies

The newest and most comprehensive studies of age-graded systems of homosexuality come to us from the South Seas, the island of New Guinea in particular, reported by anthropologists for more than one hundred years but studied intensively since the mid-1970s (Herdt 1993). Whereas age-structured homoerotic relations in most areas of the world are long gone, the result of political and religious suppression, colonization, and change, in New Guinea and the offshore islands of Melanesia these customs survived into the late twentieth century. I have described these practices among the Sambia and their sexual culture in great detail, and they are also highlighted in the film *Guardians of the Flutes,* which was filmed on location with my assistance by the British Broadcasting Corporation (1990–1993).

These comparative studies have shown the scope and symbolic significance of customary homoerotic relations between boys and men that are a part of a tradition of warriorhood, of life in gender-segregated men's clubhouses in each village, and of initiation into secret societies of and for men. The cultural practices in question have been reported since the nineteenth century and were generally referred to initially as "sodomy" or "homosexuality" and later as "ritualized homosexuality" (Herdt 1981). As evidence mounted and theory changed, however, an awareness of the pejorative meanings of the early categories, together with an understanding of the differences between homosexual as a western identity category and the New Guinea practices, gradually led me to create a cultural concept that is closer to the experience and cultural meaning of the practice in New Guinea: "boy-inseminating rituals." The new construct emphasized the belief and stated purpose of the practices, which in all known cases were not primarily to give the men pleasure, but to "grow" and "masculinize" the younger male, especially by providing his body with the semen that it could not produce on its own. This practice was intended not only to prepare the lad for warfare, and for social and reproductive competence in public and secret ritual affairs, thereby enabling him one day to marry and produce children, but also to instruct him in carrying on the sacred traditions of his ancestors.

The practice of boy-inseminating rituals is very ancient and widespread throughout this region of the world. Approximately sixty distinct precolonial cultures practiced this form of same-gender relationship in the coastal and southwestern areas of New Guinea, some of the off-lying islands of New Hebrides, and a few traditional tribal groups among the Australian Aborigines. This number represents approximately 10–20 percent of all the societies that have been systematically studied in this area. These tribal groups include the Marind-anim of southwestern Papua (now Irian Jaya, Indonesia—studied by the great Dutch anthropologist Jan van Baal 1966); the Big Nambas of New Hebrides (now Vanuatu), East Bay, Solomon Islands; and in Papua New Guinea the Sambia; the Baruya (studied by French anthropologist Maurice Godelier 1986); and the Gebusi (studied by American anthropologist Bruce Knauft 1993). These societies exist on the margins of the numerically larger Highlands New Guinea societies. Based on the turn-of-the-century writings of Alfred Haddon and Paul Wirtz and, later, Jan van Baal, anthropologists, including myself, have suggested that institutionalized same-gender practices were distinctive of a cultural migration or of waves of non-Austronesian or Papuan language groups from as much as ten thousand years ago (reviewed in Herdt 1993). Linguistic and cultural evidence, primarily in the form of word lists, diffusion of ritual practices, and morphological structural parallels of myths and legends of origin, hints that prehistoric hunter-gatherer groups migrated here and carried with them an ancient ritual complex of semen beliefs and practices not unlike those known from the Sambia.

In the worldview of many New Guinea cultures, the body and its fluids are critical for an understanding of *all* sexuality. Semen, in the local cultural model, is regarded as an elixir of life, a vital constituent of growth and well-being, and a necessary means for the production of masculinity and warriorhood personality. According to the sexual culture of such peoples as the Marind-anim, the Baruya, and the Sambia, semen as a male essential fluid is critical to the process of masculine development, on a par with the provision of blood as a female essential fluid and mother's milk in nurturing the baby. Furthermore, semen is believed to have the magical power to transform itself into mother's milk, fetal tissue, muscles, and other elements of physical and spiritual development of the growing child, much as the fertility of a garden is enhanced by the infusion of magical substances. It follows then that a number of these societies, including the Sambia, believe that only insemination will produce the desired outcome of manhood in the boy since the male body does not "naturally" create semen but rather must have it culturally implanted through the proper moral and social relations of ritual. By contrast, girls' bodies are more complete, and even though the men believe that the female body may also be strengthened and provided with breast milk through the insemination of the girl (through oral sex with her young husband), there is still a sense in these societies that the male body is deficient and the female body more complete. It is a curious issue in male-dominated cultures and has been the object of much speculation and interpretation by scholars for years.

All the New Guinea cases are organized by boy-inseminating practices that are always structured by age and are hierarchical. The older male is the penetrator and semen donor, while the younger male is always the semen recipient and is generally perceived to be more passive. In return for the gift of semen, the older male receives the gift of pleasure and no doubt the social confirmation of having achieved manhood in the eyes of his comrades' sexual culture. Since the practice is secret, the women and children are not aware of boy-inseminating, having not been initiated into the men's club. A long controversy among scholars concerns the question of whether the secret has been kept absolutely hidden or whether the women are in fact aware but are kept politically suppressed by the men's "reign of silence" (Herdt 1981). The truth is probably a mixture of both; however, careful study in some societies suggests that at least in the traditional culture women were kept out of the secrecy to a remarkable extent.

Among Australian Aborigines, the Marind-anim, the Sambia, and many other Melanesian cultures organized around boy-inseminating rituals, male/female relationships were also organized along age and hierarchy in sexual arrangements. The hierarchical nature of age-structured relations was mirrored in the fact that the girl was always expected to be several years younger than her husband. The Australian Aborigines carried this practice to its furthest extreme by a gerontocracy that in theory married young nubile girls to men the same age of the girls' grandfathers. Likewise, among the Big Nambas tribe and several other off-lying island cultures, the boy could be "married" to an older man or taken as a sexual partner by a chief one or two generations his senior. In general, these cultures could not imagine same-gender relations between equals or reciprocal sexuality between partners, either men and women or men and boys.

Several principles will help to clarify the lifeways of boy-inseminating rituals as these promote age-structured relationships throughout the region. First, everywhere in the culture area boy-inseminating relationships are implemented through initiation or puberty rites, which in general are collective, rather than individualized, ceremonies (in contrast to the two-spirit tradition among American Indians). Second, these rites always have religious sanctification in the belief that ancestral spirits or beings attend or bless the proceedings. The homoerotic is here indelibly linked to the spiritual development and afterlife of the whole person, not just to sex. Third, same-gender erotic relations are rationalized through social roles that are also age-graded and that involve entry into hierarchical secret societies. The lawful nature of these roles is specified by cultural rules according to which the boy can advance to a higher status (including war leader or elder) only through ritual and insemination. Fourth, ritual beliefs motivate and rationalize insemination as the masculine elixir vital to all physical growth, social maturity, and reproductive competence. There is no substitute for semen in this way, and therefore all males must undergo the ritual process of being inseminated when they are growing up.

Fifth, kinship and marriage and their related rights and prohibitions govern the formation of same-gender sexual relationships; for example, incest taboos mirror those of heterosexual bonds, forbidding homosexual intercourse between male relatives (father, brothers, cousins, age-mates). That these cultural ideals are sometimes broken, as they are in heterosexual incest taboos, has been documented for the Sambia, but they are broken only among cousins or distant kin, and these infractions are always hidden from the male community to avoid punishment.

Sixth, cultural ideals in some societies dictate who the preferred inseminator of the boy should be, as, for example, among the Sambia, who prefer that the older sexual partner be the boy's older brother-in-law. The reason for this preference is the marriage exchange system: The boy's family gave the gift of a woman to the other clan-family, and in return the boy should receive the gift of semen from his older sister's husband, which enables the boy to grow and become strong. In fact, of course, many other males may serve as inseminators of the boy so long as they meet the social criteria of being unrelated and fertile. Thus, a boy desires affection from an older male, who inseminates and socially supports him, all of which guarantees same-gender desires and excitements in the lifeway of these peoples. Later the older male "returns" the favor of such affections when as a man he enters into such relationships to donate his semen to a younger boy. Yet these sexual relations do not preclude interactions, including marriage and passion, with women—another kind of sexual and gender object—who may offer a different form of social achievement as well as sexual desire and excitement.

Take note that in many of these cultures the preferred and idealized object of beauty is the male, not the female, and the male is imagined as a kind of sex object, which supports the notion that a male can be an object of desire. These experiences are not partitioned in developmental and cultural reasoning as would be done in western culture. Consequently, western representations of these practices must differ from the role of "homosexual." Neither is the cultural ideal of the "bisexual" like the Melanesian practice. The western bisexual role imagines that a choice is being made between male or female partners or both, whereas in these New Guinea cultures no such choice is made: All males have sexual relations first with boys and later with women as a matter of their socially sanctioned life cycle. The New Guinea boy's developmental desires for same-gender relations in this tradition are made "real and necessary" by his culture, which cannot "work" without the institutionalization of multiple sexual subject/object relationships that lead from his childhood into old age. By contrast, western society in the modern period cannot imagine desires occurring both for males and females, with males being both the subjects and objects of older males.

Wherever mutuality existed between male sexual partners, as reported in rare cases of mutual masturbation among adolescent boys, these cultures had undergone social change and colonization that introduced new norms (Herdt 1991b). Only two exceptions have been reported in this regard. The first instance of mutualistic or egalitarian homoerotic relations was reported a generation ago by William Davenport for East Bay society, and it was later found to have been subject to social change. In a more recent example, Tobias Schneebaum reports a kind of sexual friendship between age-mates of equal age and status in Asmat society, northwest New Guinea (cited in Herdt 1991b). In my reanalysis of this case, I questioned the degree to which this partnership was traditional (Herdt 1993). It was found in both cases that colonial social change was in play. At any rate these two exceptions do not violate the general structural principle of age hierarchy in all same-gender traditional sexual relations.

Age-structured homoerotic relations between females are rare in New Guinea, and the reasons are not entirely clear. In general, as noted by other authorities (Adam 1986; Blackwood 1986; Greenberg 1988), the occurrence of female/female age structures are infrequent throughout the world, having been seldom reported from ancient societies and rarely in Melanesia (Herdt 1984a). The tentative and sketchy reports of institutionalized same-gender relations between females that we do have make it difficult to give depth and meaning to the practice, such as among the famous Big Nambas society of the New Hebrides (now Vanuatu; see Deacon 1934). In that case higher-ranking women could take younger girls as sexual partners in a kind of ritualized practice that bears comparison to the male practice, but obviously without the emphasis on semen transmission. We might speculate that male anthropologists have not been allowed into secret settings in which such practices occurred. However, in a recent and detailed sexual study of the Gimi people of New Guinea reported by a female anthropologist (Gillison 1993), male and female institutionalized homoerotic activity was absent. No doubt the issue of male domination of women and children is relevant to the cultural elaboration of boy-inseminating rites. But this does not seem to be a complete explanation, and further research is needed to explain the male and female differences.

We should note the symbolism of these boy-inseminating practices as it expresses the sexual cultures of ancient and time-honored ways of life. The stress on ritual shows the alliance between the religious forces of the society and same-gender relations both in social dominance and in religious and sexual hierarchy. In effect, homosexuality as an ideal of desiring and admiring the male body is regarded as a sort of sacred institution in some of these cultures, whereas heterosexuality is thought to belong to the secular and even polluted world. Because of the strong association between ritual purity and male insemination, there is an ideal of ritual "purity" that supports the practices. In addition, the homoerotic practices are universal for all males in the relevant societies—suggesting the symbolic theme of regeneration and rebirth through processes entirely controlled by males. As males go through these rites, the elders say that the boys are able to incorporate changes in their sexuality, again through ritual, thus enabling them to attain marriage and father children.

But these sexual behaviors are all part of their sexual lifeway and should not be thought of as individual choices or desires in the more narrow western sense. Nor must we think that the men do not receive pleasure from the practice. Clearly, sexual power and pleasure are involved, but neither of these is sufficient to explain the entire belief system and practice. A further point about the cultural ideals is how the male inseminator should be a socially appointed mentor, often the boy's brother-in-law, sometimes metaphorically referred to as mother's brother. This suggests that the boy's sister is exchanged on condition that the older male provide the gift of semen and "growth" as a compensation for the loss of female reproductive resources to the donor group. Finally, the homoerotic techniques commonly known from these New Guinea societies are confined to oral sexual relations (fellatio) and anal sex—about equally divided in the sexual practices in question in these cultures. However, two or three incidences of masturbation have been reported in which the older male is stimulated and his semen is then rubbed on the younger boy's body to stimulate growth. Curiously enough, in all known cases these sexual practices are mutually exclusive: Either a society implements oral sex, or it has anal sex; but both of them never occur within the same society. Why this is so remains a mystery (Herdt 1989).

Sexual lifeways in the boy-inseminating cultures of New Guinea created a social identity and personal network of relationships that facilitated a man having multiple desires and expressing these in sexual relations across the total course of life, from childhood to old age. These sexual lifeways allowed men to engage in same-gender relations before marriage and afterward, with exclusive relations with their wives, which created multiple desired persons as objects. Thus, sexuality was based on the experience of more than one kind of sexual desire and relationship. But change has swept most of this away. A recent survey of sexual practices in New Guinea suggests that, even though the practice of boy-inseminating rituals has largely died out, a small number of men from a health survey reported having had sex with other men, typically anal sex at the age of sixteen, often mentioning white expatriates in their stories (National Study Team 1994, 99). They did so without the support of traditional customs, such as the initiation rituals, which suggests that within a generation the forms of same-gender relations may resemble more closely the kind of gay and lesbian roles known elsewhere.

Gender-Transformed Relationships

A second form of same-gender relations involves homoerotic relations between persons based on the cultural requirement that one of the partners take on the role and dress or accoutrements of the other gender. Thus, gender here takes the place of age in the organization of the social and historical practice in select places and times. In these societies the emphasis is on one person performing the role of the "man," while the other person takes the role of the "woman." The cultural role of the genders in sex, marriage, and reproduction obviously matters in any understanding of these same-gender relations.

But geography is also significant. Age-structured systems of homoerotic relations seem to be common to the Pacific and the South Seas, whereas gender-structured systems are more widely distributed in Africa and most of the New World, including North and South

America, as well as insular Southeast Asia and the Asian mainland. As institutional forms, age-structured roles like those of New Guinea are virtually nonexistent in the New World. By contrast, gender-transformed roles are almost entirely absent from Melanesia, Aboriginal Australia, and most areas of Africa. Precisely why these geographical distributions occur in this way is widely debated among specialists (Murray 1992a).

But let us consider the variety of cultures that implement "third-gender" and "third-sex" roles. It is often questioned whether culture or whether biology causes the "reversal" of gender—from male to female or from female to male—found in traditional examples of transvestitism around the world. Western culture has generally placed exaggerated emphasis on biology, as noted in Chapter 2. But more pertinent is the issue of whether a two-sex, two-gender system is universal or whether—as occurs in a variety of nonwestern cultures—divergent roles, including third sexes and third genders, can be institutionalized. In fact, many of the examples considered here are best defined as third genders, in which the culture elaborates notions of the reality of and socialization into a third gender role—a particular kind of gendered person (neither male nor female) with symbolic qualities particular to that role.

Through the long course of generations and with sufficient historical time, the necessary presence of individuals who desire to be different and serve in third-gender and third-sex roles enables us to understand how a community might provide for these alternative sexual lifeways. For the third gender, as in the case of women who dress in men's clothes, we are dealing with biologically normative individuals who change only their role. That is, they learn the knowledge and social performance of the other gender. However, in the case of third sexes, we are dealing with individuals who are biologically hermaphroditic or who make themselves that way through cultural means, such as castration. Examples of third sexes are the famed palace eunuchs of the Byzantine Empire or classical Arabia; the Hijras of India, who are either biologically hermaphroditic at birth or undergo a castration rite in late adolescence; and the modern transsexual, a person who feels that he or she was born in the wrong body, with an identity of the other sex, and who desires sexual surgery to completely pass as the other sex. Especially in ancient societies and those organized by kinship, a social and ontological identity category clearly differentiates these individuals from those of the two genders and biological sexes.

The special form of gender in organizing homoerotic relations in most of these societies generally involves social, cultural, and psychological factors to support the appropriate sexual practices or lifeways. Our knowledge of such third-gender roles comes from the Pacific rim and the Americas, especially the two-spirit person of the North American Indians; from cross-dressing women in Europe (and, later, North America) between the fourteenth and early twentieth centuries; and from Polynesian forms of gender transformation. In virtually all of these cases, the sexual culture in question not only constructed a role for the person, but also elaborated a mythology and social practices that supported the development of the person entering that role. The person might be recruited to the role in one culture through a feeling of being "different," whereas in another a vision quest, desires of the family, or decisions of religious groups were the key in recruitment procedures and socialization opportunities. Special rules or norms were created to support the social performance, such as the Mojave initiation of the two spirit or third gender at age ten or the Navajo fertility magic controlled by the two-spirit person. Whatever the case, these dramatic and often mythologized roles permitted the expression of homoerotic desires and passions and partnerships of a significant order not entirely removed from the ideas of lesbian and gay roles as these are known today.

Native North America

Of all the worldwide examples of third genders, none is better known than the form that so widely occurred among precolonial American Indian tribes. A new view of this so-called two-spirit person (formerly known as a *berdache*) or man-woman is now gaining recognition in anthropology and the cultural history of sexuality. The term *berdache*, now in disfavor, was borrowed by the French, among others, from the Arabic *bardaj*, a male, possibly a slave, who had passive sexual relations with another man who dominated him.

Typically, *berdache* was invoked by colonial or missionary authorities as a slur on the honor and customs of native peoples. Aside from
this sexual chauvinism, *berdache* was reductionistic because its connotations were only sexual and thereby lacked the social or spiritual
meanings of such importance in Native American groups. Consequently, current authorities prefer to use man-woman or two-spirit
concepts, and I myself prefer the latter because of the religious and
spiritual importance accorded to the role in these societies. This is
not to deny the love, sex, and passion involved, only to expand on
the notions of the past, which regarded same-gender relationship as
having to do only with sex.

Recent study demonstrates both how widespread and well accepted was the two-spirit role in more than one hundred American
Indian tribes. In all of these tribes, men took on the role, while in approximately one-third, particularly among hunting and gathering
groups, women took on the role as well (Blackwood 1986; Williams
1986). Anthropologists widely debate why the male role was more
common than the female one, though we generally agree that social
power and gender role requirements play a critical part in the answer (Roscoe 1994). Certainly, each community's local theory of
gender may have been involved since among some peoples, such as
the Zuni Indians of the southwestern United States, gender was
more of an acquired than a learned complex of features (Roscoe
1991). Some have suggested that the two-spirit role was ridiculed or
stigmatized, but it has been effectively shown that among such
American groups as the Navajo, the two spirit enjoyed high status,
and what looked like ridicule was a form of joking found among
other social categories as well (Greenberg 1988).

In these cultures the role of the two spirit was so ceremonialized
and had such a high profile that even ordinary people could say who
would become a two spirit. The role enabled successful performance
of gender tasks and roles without the person being that biological
sex. The personal name would be changed from a man's to a
woman's, or vice versa, and the two spirit would succeed in passing
as a man or a woman among strangers. The transformation of the biological male into a two spirit would be complete when he/she would
do housekeeping, crafts, and gardening and handle household and fi-

nancial affairs typically managed by women. Potential two spirits were identified by their initiation into the role; their knowledge of its myths and customs; their occupational preference for the role of the other gender, often beginning in childhood; their skill as a storyteller or healer; their dressing and appearing in accoutrements of the other gender; their emotions and mannerisms, which appeared to be more like those of the other gender; and their preference for homoerotic relations, apparently expressed as a desire for same-gender partnerships in adult life. Since gender roles did not always determine sexual relations in these tribes, questions of the ultimate sexual orientations and relations of the two spirits remain unclear.

One of the most remarkable examples of a two spirit was the famed Zuni Indian personality known as We'wha, a biological male who lived in the clothes and role of women but also held power in the greatest of the Zuni councils (Roscoe 1990, 29ff). We'wha, a man who transformed into the third-gender role called *lhamana*, was adventurous, progressive, and shrewd; he fascinated the most sophisticated urban society of the times. Already by age "three or four, We'wha had revealed his inclinations to being an *lhamana*. He wanted to put on girls clothes; he liked to clean the house and cook and so on, as his family explained" (Roscoe 1990, 33). Sexual experimentation was widely tolerated among the Zuni, and We'wha engaged in homoerotic relations with boys and men, although perhaps not exclusively. So successful was We'wha in passing as female that he was presented to high society in Washington, D.C., as an "Indian Princess" and is reported to have been the first two spirit to have ever shaken hands with a president of the United States, who in 1886 was Grover S. Cleveland (Roscoe 1990, 70–71). We'wha seems to have secured the reputation of the Zuni as the peaceful friend and ally of the United States on the New Mexico frontier of the times.

The two-spirit role may have reached a high point in its cultural elaboration among the Mojave Indians on the desert border of California and Arizona. The Mojave were a highly sex-positive people, known for their forthright and open way of discussing sexuality. They were remarkable in having sanctioned both male (*alyha*) and female (*hwame*) two-spirit roles, each of which had its own distinctive social positions and worldviews. The *alyha* preferred the occupations of women and homoerotic relations with men. The *hwame* was a manly hearted woman who enjoyed the pursuits of men and the pleasures and domestic companionship of women.

The mythological importance of these two-spirit roles in the creation of the whole culture and its sexual lifeways was anchored in Mojave origin myths. According to them, the first *alyha* had to undergo a series of ordeals, and body painting, to overcome the shame of transforming from one role to other. But as all the people assisted in the ceremony, the shame was abolished, and the man-woman, dressed, speaking, and laughing as a woman, participated in public festivities and brought good fortune to the people. The story reminds us of the incredible power of culture to support and validate a sexual lifeway, making of what at first seemed shameful an honorable and even admired way of being human. In Chapter 4 we study more closely the initiation customs that led the Mojave boy to become a two spirit and why the role bears comparison to alternative lifeways elsewhere.

The Mojave two-spirit male took on not only the social roles but also the biological-symbolic functions of women. The man-woman clearly enjoyed the sense of having reproductive functions. He/she performed all of the common household tasks of a woman, much like the Zuni two spirit did, but the Mojave liked the dramatic, had a flair for it, and went even further. Thus, in addition to having a female name, he/she would also enact the regular menstrual periods of a woman by scratching between his/her legs to create blood. He/she would then retire for some time in the manner typical of menstruating women. He/she would also on occasion imitate childbirth by ingesting local plants that created prolonged constipation, ultimately being unloaded as a newborn "child." The sexual excitement of the two spirit—who had male genitals—was very specific to a kind of homoeroticism. It was the man-woman's desire to be penetrated anally and in this way to achieve an ejaculation while the male partner—the man—was inside of him/her. Likewise, the woman-man would have sex by rubbing her vulva against the woman partner, with the two spirit on top, to orgasm. Marriage and partnership between a two spirit and an ordinary person were recognized, and adoption was sometimes achieved to create a full family. Likewise, the manly hearted woman was known to have children with (but not procreated by) her partner.

The study of the two spirit was for many years mired in problems of western ethnocentrism and sexual chauvinism that derived from our own model of homosexuality as a disease. A case in point is a classic study of the Mojave Indians conducted by George Devereux (1937), a brilliant and eccentric scholar, friend of the Mojave, but dogmatic advocate of psychoanalysis. Devereux's work in the mid-1930s provides the richest description of the time, but it is biased and at times simply wrong in its interpretations, as revealed by his own evidence (Herdt 1991a). Devereux could never shake himself of all the negative meanings of homosexuality, and he confused the homosexual role with the Mojave two-spirit role, revealing for all time the dangers of mixing two different cultures and confusing one culture's ideas about sexuality and gender with another's. The Mojave did not have rigid male/female dualisms and were by western standards very approving of same-gender desires and indeed of sexual experimentation and alternative sexualities. Devereux could not understand this. The exceptional and unusual individuals who elected to become two spirits were generally permitted to do so with minimum social pressure. But the model used by Devereux pins them rigidly into a Freudian system that describes them as "inverted," "abnormal," "crazy"—as deviant in some way. The lesson from Devereux's study is that even the brilliance of a gifted mind could not overcome the heavy prejudices of western culture and psychoanalysis in its distorted picture of same-gender relations across cultures.

Two-spirit people in many times and places were thought to have magical or healing abilities and in the spiritual realm to be quite powerful. Among the Navajo Indians, who regarded the man-woman as a good omen, the two spirit was believed to bring blessings of fertility to the land and the people and was even compared at the time to the admired President Franklin D. Roosevelt of the United States—a sort of "good luck charm"! Much of the opposition of the early white settlers on the American frontier to the *berdache* was focused on the "sexual inversion" of the role. These westerners largely ignored spiritual aspects of this third gender throughout Native North American tribes. They did not seem to understand that this was a part of the aboriginal religion in this part of the world. This was a grave error because the religious aspect of the two spirit was highly important and in the spiritual realm the two spirits were powerful. Among the Mojave, a divine aspect of the homoerotic desires of the two spirit surfaces repeatedly in the tribe's beliefs about myth and dreams. While pregnant, the mothers of two spirits dreamed that their offspring would become neither men nor women. This omen more than anything else may have created in the parents and community a future potential for accepting the children's nature as that of man-woman. Creation myths mention their initiation. Such a sacred charter for the divinely inspired nature explains much of the two spirits' general social acceptance in local groups, as Walter Williams (1986) has noted in his survey. Two spirits were also lucky at gambling, an omen of glad tidings to which the Navajo, in their culture, were especially attracted. And two spirits were exceptionally powerful shamans, particularly the female two spirit.

If we compare the Mojave category of two spirit with the turn-of-the-century homosexual inversion role as specified in Chapter 2, several critical differences emerge. First, the Mojave Indians viewed gender transformation as a part of the whole person; they did not privilege some kind of biology or existential choice in the matter. However, they did go so far as to expect the individual to express his or her desires for transformation in late childhood at the time of the initiation customs (see Chapter 4). Second, the Mojave ascribed to the ontological nature of the two-spirit person certain gifted, unusual, or aberrant characteristics that included the symbolic production of the reproductive functions of the other gender. In this way, even though the Mojave provided for a third gender, they did not entirely escape placing emphasis on reproduction in the "female role." Third, by agreeing with the cultural reassignment of the man-woman to his/her chosen sex, and by using the appropriate referential pronouns—"she" rather than "he" (or vice versa in the case of a woman-man)—they confirmed a subjective identity state, similar to the recent experience of the western transsexual (Stoller 1985). Fourth, the Mojave acknowledged that the sexual excitement of the two spirit was directed at the same gender but with the twist that only by serving as a third gender could a two spirit achieve sexual relations with someone of the same sex.

This combination of traits came close to providing homoerotic relations with a "natural and normal" expression in American Indian cultures, so long as the rules of the two-spirit role were observed. The cultural reality attributes of the role coexisted with moral attributions of a somewhat pejorative kind among some of these groups. Yet even though two-spirit people were at times teased or mildly disparaged, their partners were never exposed to stigma or any form of negative social visibility as far as is known (Williams 1986). That their partners were never stigmatized for having sex with a two spirit was a critical sign of social acceptance of these relationships in the community. What mattered in these sexual cultures was not the sex acts or the gender of the person but their expression in terms of the institutional role of being in a third gender. In this regard, it seems to me, the American Indians' lifeways humanized the moral condition of same-gender relations far more than did western society in prior periods.

Although more is known of the male than of the female transformation into being a third gender or a two-spirit person, for some girls and women in many traditional cultures (Blackwood 1986) this was a significant social role. Locals thought that even before birth the two spirit could be intuited in the womb of the mother, as, for example, among the Mojave *hwame,* who is said to have dreamed of becoming cross-gender while still in the womb. In other groups, fasting and vision quests or divination formed the basis on which a woman might be called to the role of two spirit.

The female two spirit often showed a desire for male pursuits and tasks in childhood. She may have played with boys and made bows and arrows for play hunting, ultimately being accepted as a legitimate holder of the two-spirit role. After puberty the woman-transformed-into-man would take a wife in the marriage market so as not to suffer a loss of status in her "male role." She would also enact the demands of the male gender role, including such activities as hunting and waging war, dressing in male clothes, and meeting the variety of male ritual obligations of the community. She might even rise to stature as a shaman, though typically she simply rose in spiritual stature, and might achieve fame as a warrior in battle. Although biologically normal, these women-men did not bear children because of their social role. Regarding their sexual behavior, we do know that among the Mojave Indians at least, the woman-man and her woman partner were said by locals to have pleasurable sexual relations accompanied by affection.

Today the role of the two spirit is very different from before, the result of colonization of American Indians, intolerance toward gays, and an absence of any kind of "universal gay community" among Indians, among other issues that represent great change in the twentieth century (Lang 1996). Many American Indians today value their cultural heritage above their sexual orientation, including the attempt to claim a two-spirit identity. There also remains the threat of AIDS/HIV, the continuing spread of which endangers the sexual openness of the two spirit. Among the most difficult persons for anthropologists and other researchers to contact are biological females who have an affinity with woman-man two-spirit roles. However, the effort to reach them is very great, pointing out once again that the anthropology of same-gender relations is a challenge and requires the greatest patience and humility (Lang 1996).

Gender-transformed roles and homoerotic relationships in the New World can be found in parts of South and Central America. Traditional practices in such complex and modernizing countries as Mexico and Brazil are dealt with in Chapter 5. The colonial history of the Spanish in particular seems replete with examples of homophobia and punishment of homosexual behavior (Williams 1986, 134ff). In ancient Peru and in Mexico the native traditions were richly endowed with erotic art, including homoerotic images. Temples and sacred art depicted same-gender sexual relations that shocked the Spanish conquistadors because they went so much against Spanish Catholic conceptions of gender and "natural" sexual relations between men and women.

The church in the early part of this historical period tended to regard same-gender relations between men as sodomy, an act of evil that approached satanism and might be thought of as witchcraft, punishable by death. This sodomy presented a moral problem to the Spanish and Portuguese friars, who in some senses were agents of the Inquisition, even in the New World. Yet cross-dressing was common in some areas, and the presence of a third gender was likely. The opposition of the priests to these forms of "evil" thus justified for the colonizing country the conquest and destruction of these native cultures, even as it meant that local customs of "sodomy" among the Indians were being systematically wiped out. Much of these ancient and noble practices of the great civilizations of the Americas have vanished along with their gods and myths. But examples of gender-transformed sexuality are still to be found.

A contemporary example of gender transformation is provided by Isthmus Zapotec society in southern Mexico. Certain feminine males, known as *muxe*, or in Spanish, *efeminado*, are known from early in their lives, sometimes as early as six months, as being "different." These third genders are unlike their male peers in seeking the company and routines of women in the household. They are reported to prefer being with other *muxe* or with girls, not with boys. Rather than follow their male relatives into the fields and other manly pastimes, they enjoy what women do—baking bread, making decorations and embroidery, and learning how to mold pottery in the manner of master artists who are *muxe* or women. They are reported to be indistinguishable from women in adulthood in terms of their posture, body movements, carriage, and so on (Royce 1987). From other reports it is clear that same-gender sexual relationships are relatively common in the area, even if many homosexuals are treated roughly or unfairly, called *puto* (whore), and forced to lived secretly, at least insofar as they might openly display their loves and desires. Here, too, AIDS is beginning to take its toll, especially among transvestites and people such as the *muxe* who would take the anally receptive role in sexual relations. The lives of these people, like those of gays and lesbians in the United States, are being forever changed by the epidemic disease (Wilson 1995). But there is hope because in the emerging gay and lesbian communities of Mexico and its neighbors a role known as the *internacional*, which is more egalitarian (like the American gay role), is now present. The *internacional* is beginning to include lesbians as well. These roles are increasing sources of sociopolitical support in sex education and prevention efforts in Mexico (Carrier 1995).

Polynesian Societies

Stories of close same-gender friendships in Polynesia, including Tahiti in the Society Islands and ancient Hawaii, were already well known by the later part of the eighteenth century. These friendships provided sources of support for same-sex relationships in a variety of Polynesian societies, which tended to be highly ranked or stratified. Women were high status, kin groups held distinctions, royalty and high chiefs were known, and these and other features made the existence of third genders a part of the social landscape. By contrast, age-structured homoerotic roles and relations of the kind we have seen in New Guinea and Africa were rare or unknown. Polynesian hierarchical systems associated social status and power with marriage and sexuality, not age.

Men who engaged in the work, roles, and sexuality of women were known from precolonial times in a variety of Polynesian societies (Besnier 1994). The high status of women in certain Polynesian cultural systems, along with the general societal approval of sexuality and sexual experimentation in childhood, certainly influenced this elaboration of gender-transformed roles. Roles in which men transformed to a third gender were the most common.

Even in the time of Captain James Cook in old Hawaii, the existence of third genders was noted. The cultural role of *aikane* was valued by the Hawaiians, including the king of Hawaii (Morris 1992), as a closely knit and intimate form of same-gender friendship that typically involved sexual relations. Both myth and history validated the importance of these traditions in the island. By the time of Captain Cook's arrival in 1778, the existence of the *aikane* suggested social roles and sexual relations as well as social values of special same-gender friendship. Cohabitation between the *aikane* was possible. Persons who enacted these relations could have spiritual power, or *mana*; could have high social status; and could participate in sacred rituals—all qualities of being well regarded in the society of the times. In the poetic language of ancient Hawaii, it was said that "an *aikane* is a nest of fragrance" (cited in Morris 1992, 95). The *aikane* were despised by certain westerners for the practice of sodomy and considered wicked and sinful by the missionaries.

Such third-gender social roles are known from a variety of Polynesian societies, and they often feature gender-transformed practices and relationships (Morris 1992). The best-known example comes from Tahiti and has been known for centuries: the *mahu*, a kind of third gender, but without the full complement of dressing or acting as the other sex, at least in contemporary times, where some of them are nightclub performers in Papeete, the capitol city. Traditionally, most of the *mahu* seem to have been males, but stories suggest that in more outlying areas there were women who desired the same gender and acted differently. Indeed, reports of such women still come from the remote islands near Tonga (Besnier 1994).

As a young child, a boy may have begun to take on characteristics of the women's role and tasks around the house. He may have taken a woman's job later in life. Some *mahu*, however, seem to have been more like other men and not so womanly in their appearance or practices. As a *mahu*, the individual took on not only the woman's daily role but also her part in traditional dances, songs, and festivals. Although the *mahu* was sometimes an object of joking and pranks, he was nevertheless a sexual partner of many of the same men who made fun of him in public; and the *mahu* were fully accepted in Tahitian society. The *mahu* were often known to enjoy same-gender sexual relations as adolescents and as adults. The typical form practiced was oral sex, in which the *mahu* would fellate his partner; there did not seem to be much, if any stigma, attached to this practice, particularly if it was clear that the other man did not suck the *mahu*. But there are also stories told in which the partners might turn around and want to fellate the *mahu* as well.

The traditional *mahu* role has in recent years undergone change. Today the male who becomes and acts as a *mahu* might be seen as another kind of transvestite, a person who dresses in the clothes and makeup of women. The practices of song and dance, of storytelling in which the *mahu* excelled, are now undergoing change in Tahiti and the surrounding island societies in which the role was always known. The transvestitism has in recent decades become a cultural object, almost a commodity, made into beauty pageants, tourist shows, and nightclub acts; occasionally this transvestitism is associated with prostitution. Ironically, this might result in a new kind of assertion of "heterosexuality," of *mahu* taking women's roles in an imagined hierarchical way quite foreign to Tahiti but in keeping with the import of certain tokens of modernity. In extreme cases it seems that some contemporary *mahu* think of having sex-change operations and becoming more like western transgendered persons or transsexuals. In traditional Polynesian culture, however, much of these practices were of a playful friendship and close sexual relationship. They involved the full social and spiritual life of the person and the special ritual role of being able to transform the self and possibly to transform things more generally. This might be thought of as a ritual transitionality, or a kind of liminal quality, in the sense that it connoted a being and becoming that were between social states (Besnier 1994). At any rate the *mahu* was someone whose social being was on occasion dramatic and fun-loving and full of life.

It is not clear that all of the individuals who were thought to be *mahu* in old Polynesia were homosexual in the sense that they generally or exclusively preferred the same gender for romance and sexual relations. Certainly, their male partners were expected to marry and have children. It is possible that some of the *mahu* were what we might call bisexual—attracted primarily to the other gender but still on occasion desiring their own gender and performing the *mahu* role. Some authorities believe that the *mahu* functioned primarily to support the local masculine/feminine gender role dichotomy in social, economic, and political activities. In this view, each traditional village had the customary role of one *mahu* who served to clarify and define the masculine model, a powerful reminder of a negative role model of what *not to be* for the other men (Levy 1973). No doubt the *mahu* may have served this function for some men on some occasions, but we must not forget that in general Tahitian society accepted the role, and there was a sense in which the gender roles and hierarchies could not work without it.

Some Tahitians fear that the *mahu* role may entirely disappear in favor of a more western-type homosexuality, in part associated with the high incidence of tourism, including tours of gays and lesbians from the United States, Australia, and Europe. This concern may be premature, however; for we must not forget that the role of becoming a *mahu* in the traditional village probably still has its counterpart today. The *mahu* remains viable and important to the continuing legacy of the distinctive customs and tolerance of these famous island societies.

Role-Structured Relations

A variety of societies are known to prescribe same-gender homoerotic relations based not on age or gender but on the successful performance of a particular specialized social role. These relationships have occurred in many cultures, with both ritual and secular forms, the best known from the ancient world being a tradition of ritual cults that provided for male or female temple prostitution to same or other-gender partners (Greenberg 1988). Both ancient and early modern society instances of role-specialized homoeroticism often appear to overlap with gender-defined or transformed homosexuality, and indeed, some of these cases make classification very difficult (Murray 1992a). Certain role-specialized examples, such as hermaphrodites or castrates, eunuchs, or the Hijras of India (see Chapter 5), might well be considered third sexes or third genders.

However, what distinguishes the sexual cultures and lifeways considered here from those of the third sexes is that in each instance the person's entry into the role is restricted. Not just anyone can attain the role, and some people may feel compelled to enact it even though doing so goes against their inner desires or their family's wishes. Furthermore, some of these societies may prohibit homosexuality or sanction it; but they actually require performance of the role, based on social and symbolic criteria, ritual practices, or dramatic performances not generally permitted or approved for other members of the society.

Historical Cases

In the modern period of western civilization, the idea of a special role for homosexuality may be easiest to identify historically with the theater. The role of the theater actor from early times on seemed to involve a good deal of role-playing and cross-dressing by boys and men taking women's roles, in spite of the fact that in secular life such cross-dressing might have been severely punished. I have already noted from other civilizations, including Edo Japan and ancient Korea, the popularity of "theater homosexuality," particularly as inscribed in boys or men dressing as girls or women and taking feminine roles onstage. In Shakespeare's time, the theater may have produced sexual contexts and role-playing in which gender transformation and the expression of desires for the same gender were regarded as fairly common occurrences. They still were not entirely approved in the theater, however, and were disapproved in public affairs (Smith 1991). But this symbolic field is not the same as the role of the homosexual, and it certainly differs from gay and lesbian roles, which had to await emancipation from political oppression well into the later twentieth century.

Another source of imagery that may have linked individual sexual identity with desires for the same gender was present in the role of the artist. It has been suggested that the earliest homoerotic role specialization of this kind might be found in the social niche of the artist in eighteenth-century England (Trumbach 1994). Here, a variety of ideas about the special nature or character of the writer, poet, and painter combined with the formation of a kind of network of hidden or marginal same-gender relations (see Chapter 6).

A more exotic form of role specialization can be found in the famed eunuchs of early civilizations and court societies, from Persia and South Asia to the Byzantine Empire in the East (Ringrose 1994). These were males whose genitals were removed or castrated for one or another purpose, such as to serve as special court officials, harem guards, or spiritually sacred healers and magicians. Originally they were feared or despised, even regarded as bad omens, as the Greeks in general did of castrates in the time of Alexander the Great. It is believed that on his conquest, however, Alexander took the favorite castrate of the defeated caliph and made the beautiful Bagoas—a eunuch—his lover. But the Greeks regarded this person as subhuman, and it remains one of history's great "imponderables" (to use Mary Renault's term) what influence, aside from his renowned beauty, Bagoas had over Alexander.

A later historical example comes from well into the Middle Ages. We know that for almost one thousand years in the Byzantine Empire there were biologically normal males who became eunuchs, who were scribes, servants, guards, and, later, high officials of the imperial courts. The transformation from male into this specialized role was not the result of an essential desire to have a female body or of a need for sexual relations with males. Instead, these persons and their families sought the prestige and privilege of the eunuch in the Byzantine court (Ringrose 1994). In the early period of the Byzantine, these castrates were of low status and were even laughed at; they may have come from poor backgrounds, and their entry into the role was considered a definite social advancement—though they paid a heavy price for it in the loss of their genitals. Eunuchs had their critics and defenders; philosophical and religious experts debated whether eunuchs' condition should be at all considered "natural." But what is natural? one of their defenders asked. No clear answer could be given, and the rule of ambiguity commenced its reign.

In later centuries, however, especially after the year 1000, the eunuchs achieved considerably higher status. In fact, one among them even became a leading general, bringing glory to his kind. For a long time his fame was held up as evidence of the need for the castrates and their abilities to surpass the status of slaves. Castrates survived into modern Europe, serving both in the famed Vienna choir and in the Sistine Chapel, until such practices were halted as barbarous in the last century.

Among the least-known historical examples involving specialized roles for homoerotic relations is the tradition of female transvestitism in early modern Europe (Dekker and van de Pol 1989). Women who dressed in men's clothes, took on their roles, and became the lovers of other women were largely secret and hidden from history, but surely some became famous, and even infamous, at certain places and times—perhaps as early as the sixteenth century, but certainly in the seventeenth and eighteenth centuries. Among the most striking stories that come down to us is a 1769 report of a woman, christened Maria van Antwerpen, who was condemned in the Dutch town of Gouda for "gross and excessive fraud in changing her name and quality . . . mocking holy and human laws concerning marriage" (Dekker and van de Pol 1989, 1). For eight years this woman had lived as a man, had enlisted as a soldier, had been conformable in dressing and riding as a man, and had successfully courted and married another woman. She was reviled and became a symbol of the subversive in many places in the ensuing years, but there was perhaps a hint of popularity and daring as well—not all of it bad, as celebrated in children's songs and lewd jokes that implicitly mocked the gender roles of the times.

Women who dressed as men were known to do so from a time when the appearance of being a man gave them a larger measure of security in traveling the highways. Even nobility was given to the practice. Eventually, however, some women successfully passed in such male roles as sailor or soldier, though the intimate quarters of a ship made such a pose difficult, and many a story tells of the misadventures and fortunes of women who passed as sailors or were discovered as permanent cross-dressers. Women took the names of men and did their best to effect the appearance or rugged looks of men. In the case of the exposed Maria, for instance, a fragment of a ballad that immortalized her looks has survived in the following verse:

> *A pearl, she stood there*
> *Before her captain's stare,*
> *And he thought he could swear*
> *He ne'er seen a lad so fair.* (Dekker and van de Pol 1989, 17)

After Maria's discovery, she wrote an autobiography in which she asserted that she would try again to enter the army, which she indeed managed to do some eleven years later.

Sexual relations between a woman dressing as a man and other women were known by the term *tribady,* the counterpart of sodomy, which was punishable and highly taboo in the eighteenth century. By contrast with female/female relationships, these relations were regarded as a more serious matter, as capable of inspiring love and sexuality, and deep partnerships, for years. But not all the women who dressed as men were entirely satisfied with the change in roles. For example, a woman known as Cornelia Gerrits is said to have so hated male clothes that even her marriage as a man to a woman was not enough to keep Gerrits from changing her role "back into a woman" (Dekker and van de Pol 1989, 58). Apparently, her disgust for male clothes made her change her mind about being a man.

Women in western Europe who dressed in men's clothes provide the basis for an understanding of a somewhat more exotic but closely allied historical form: the so-called Sworn Virgins of Albania and related mannish women in the Balkans, known since the nineteenth century (Gremaux 1994). These were women who took on the dress and masculine roles of men and seemed so mannish that they were rather easily incorporated into the highly dualistic sexual cultures of the area. Of course, much European folklore, Balkan included, describes female cross-dressing and provides stories of the military exploits of female cross-dressers, as we have seen.

The sense of this specialized role is enhanced by the idea of the Sworn Virgins of Albania—women who vowed to remained virgins, or social virgins, throughout their lives, which strongly implied that they would neither marry men nor have sex with men. This distinction between a "woman" and a "virgin" is symbolically fascinating. On occasion, the circumstances of a particular family and kinship, and the preservation of family honor and estate, apparently dictated that a certain girl would take on this role. Such families seemed to promote the idea, although it was typically a secret role specialization. Not every woman was capable of being a celibate sworn virgin; this seems to have been the special combination of a girl's nature and the wishes of the family. True to the Slavic customs of the times, these women-men were expert hunters and woodsmen, with a passion for shooting. They tended to prefer the company of men, to converse and play cards with them, and in certain cases to take on the misogynist attitudes of the men. Manliness seemed second nature to these women-men. Whether sexual behavior with others of the same gender ever occurred seems doubtful, as a breaking of the vow of celibacy could result in death by stoning. The ethnographer who studied this phenomenon himself reported that local people were surprised by his interest in the matter. They said to him: "What is so exceptional about them that you have come all this way? After all, they are not women but virgins!" (Gremaux 1994, 281).

Among the best-known precolonial instance of specialized third-gender roles that required religious recruitment and approved homoerotic relations as a function of the role is the famed shaman of Chukchi (Tungus) in northeastern Siberia (Herdt 1987a; Murray

1992a). The subjective and cultural report of this role comes from the exquisite early ethnography of the Russians, whose writings provided the basic understanding of this complex form of shamanism and role-specialized homoeroticism. If we were to go so far as to agree with the notable scholar of comparative religion Mircea Eliade (1951), we might call this a kind of "divine or religious homosexuality," and indeed, it would be among the most distinctive examples of such from tribal societies. What is remarkable is the report of men who become shamans through a "spiritual calling" to the role, eventually leading them, seemingly against their will or desires, to cross-dress and take same-gender partners.

In general, Chukchi sexual culture did not approve of homosexuality, nor did it have any other institutional means for its expression. However, the practice of shamanism involved spirit familiars, dreams and omens, and many kind of rituals directed toward healing the sick and restoring their souls. For this reason the role specialization was much needed and admired. The shaman's position was believed to be determined by the spirits and fates. They "called" the man to the role of healer, and their powers enabled him to engage in magical flight, exorcism, and other shamanistic functions. At the beginning the man was led into a kind of vision quest, which might bring on spirit possession of his body. At times the spirits might call on him to change gender and take up a third-gender sexuality. Certain shamans even publicly complained of this fate, grudgingly accepting their homoerotic calling for the good of society. Surely we might call this the earliest form of altruistic homosexuality known!

The Chukchi shaman's role required same-gender relations in a society that did not otherwise recognize or approve them. The ritual quest was directly involved in the gender change. To make a very powerful incantation, the shaman had to strip himself naked and go out into the night. He would undergo ceremonies that, it was believed, transformed his body, even his genitals, into a "softer sex." Afterward, his fate secured, he would dress in a woman's clothes and act in certain respects like a woman. This man-woman was thought then to lose masculine strength and his abilities at male pursuits, such as hunting, and instead to become healing and nurturing in the way of acting and talking like a woman. The man-woman might in time take lovers and, if circumstances permitted, eventually arrange for marriage to a man, following the usual rituals. The vows of the couple would last until death. The shaman's husband would perform the male duties, and the new "wife" would tend the house and engage in the various obligations of a woman, including sexual intercourse, with the husband acting as the active inseminator in anal sex. I regard this example as paradigmatic for all role-specialized homosexuality.

◄ 4 ►

Coming of Age and
Coming Out Ceremonies
Across Cultures

COMING OF AGE AND BEING socialized into the sexual lifeways of the culture through ceremonies and initiation rites are common in many cultures of the world. These traditions help to incorporate the individual—previously a child, possibly outside of the moral rules and sexual roles of the adult group—into the public institutions and practices that bring full citizenship. We have seen in prior chapters many examples of these transitions and ceremonial practices, and we are certainly justified in thinking of them as basic elements in the human condition. Coming of age or "puberty" ceremonies around the world are commonly assumed to introduce the young person to sexual life as a heterosexual. In both traditional and modern societies, ritual plays a role in the emergence of sexuality and the support of desires and relationships expected in later life.

Yet not all of this is seamless continuity, and in the study of homosexuality across cultures we must be aware of the gaps and barriers that exist between what is experienced in childhood or adolescence and the roles and customs in adulthood that may negate or oppose these experiences. Ruth Benedict (1938) stresses how development in a society may create cultural discontinuities in this sexual and gender cycle of identities and roles, necessitating rituals. She hints that homosexuality in particular may cause discontinuity of this kind, and the life stories of many gays and lesbians in western society reveal this problem. But in all societies, there is an issue of connecting childhood with adulthood, with the transition from sexual or biological immaturity to sexual maturity. In short, these transitions may create a "life crisis" that requires a social solution—and this is the aim of initiation ceremonies and rites of transition. Rituals may provide for the individual the necessary means to achieve difficult changes in sexual and gender status. Particularly in deeply emotional rituals, the energy of the person can be fully invested or bonded to the newfound group. This may create incredible attachments of the kind we have observed among the ancient Greeks, the feudal Japanese, and the Sambia of New Guinea, wherein the younger boy is erotically involved or partnered with an older male. In the conditions of a warrior society, homoerotic partnerships are particularly powerful when they are geared to the survival of the group.

The transition out of presumptive heterosexuality and secrecy and into the active process of self-identifying as gay or lesbian in the western tradition bears close comparison with these rites of passage. In the process of "coming out"—the current western concept of ritual passage—as gay or lesbian, a person undergoes emotional changes and a transformation in sexuality and gender that are remarkable and perhaps equal in their social drama to the initiation rites of small societies in New Guinea and Africa. Thus, the collective aspirations and desires of the adolescent or child going through the ritual to belong, participate in, and make commitments to communities of his or her own kind take on a new and broader scope.

Coming out is an implicit rite of passage for people who are in a crisis of identity that finds them "betwixt and between" being presumed to be heterosexual and living a totally secret and hidden life as a homosexual. Not until they enter into the gay or lesbian lifeway or the sexual culture of the gay and lesbian community will they begin to learn and be socialized into the rules, knowledge, and social roles and relationships of the new cultures. For many people, this experience is liberating; it is a highly charged, emotional, and dramatic process that changes them into adult gays or lesbians in all areas of their lives—with biological families, with coworkers, with friends or schoolmates, and with a sexual and romantic partner of the same gender, possibly for the rest of their lives.

This transformation in the self and in social relations brings much that is new and sometimes frightening. An alternative moral system is opened up by the rituals. Why people who desire the same gender require a ritual when others in our society do not is painfully clear. Ritual is necessary because of the negative images, stigma, and intense social contamination that continue to exist in the stereotypes and antihomosexual laws of our society. To be homosexual is to be discredited as a full person in society; it is to have a spoiled identity—as a homosexual in society or as a frightened closet homosexual who may be disliked by openly gay and lesbian friends. But perhaps of greatest importance are the repression and social censorship involved: to have one's desires suppressed, to even experience the inner or "true" self as a secret.

It is hard to break through this taboo alone or without the support of a community because doing so exposes the person to all sorts of risk, requires considerable personal resources, and precipitates an emotional vulnerability that for many is very difficult to bear. But that is not all. For some people in our society, homosexuality is a danger and a source of pollution. Once the person's homosexuality is revealed, the stigma can also spread to the family, bringing the pollution of shame and dishonor to father and mother, clan and community. This is the old mask of the evil of homosexuality that we explored in Chapter 2. And this is what we have found in a study of these matters in Chicago (Herdt and Boxer 1996).

It is very typical to see an intense and negative reaction of family members to the declaration of same-sex desires by adolescents, even this late in the twentieth century. Society changes slowly and its myths even more slowly. For many people, homosexuality is an evil as frightening to the imagination as the monsters of bad Hollywood movies. Many people find it extremely difficult to deal with homosexuality and may exert strong pressures on their young to hide and suppress their feelings. Consequently, young people may feel that by declaring their same-sex desires, they will betray their families or the traditions of their sexual culture and its lifeways, which privilege marriage and the carrying on of the family name. And the younger person who desires the same gender may be afraid to come out for fear of dishonoring his or her ethnic community in the same way. To prevent these reactions, many people—closet homosexuals in the last century and many who fear the effects today—hide their basic feelings and all of their desires from their friends and families.

Here is where we may learn a lesson from other cultures. The mechanism of ritual helps to teach about the trials and ordeals of passages in other times and places, which in itself is a comfort, for it signals something basic in the human condition. To come out is to openly challenge sexual chauvinism, homophobia, and bias—refusing to continue the stigma and pollution of the past and opening new support and positive role models where before there were none. Through examples from New Guinea, the Mojave, and the Chicago gay and lesbian group, I examine these ideas in the following pages.

Many cultures around the world celebrate coming of age with a variety of events and rituals that introduce the person to sexual life. Indeed, initiation can be an introduction to sexual development and erotic life (Hart 1963). In Aboriginal Australia and New Guinea wherever the precolonial secret societies of the region flourished, the nature of all sexual interaction was generally withheld from prepubertal boys and girls until initiation. It often began their sense of sexual being, even if they had not achieved sexual puberty, since maturation often occurred late in these societies. Many of the Pacific societies actually disapproved of childhood sexual play, for this was felt to disrupt marriage and social regulation of premarital social relations. The Sambia are no different, having delayed sexual education until the initiation of boys and girls in different secret contexts for each. The stories of Sambia boys are clear in associating the awakening of their sexuality in late childhood with their initiation rites and fellatio debut with adolescent bachelor partners. The definition of social reality was thus opened up to same-gender sexuality.

Sambia Boys' Ritual Initiation

The Sambia are a tribe numbering more than two thousand people in the Eastern Highlands of Papua New Guinea. Most elements of culture and social organization are constructed around the nagging destructive presence of warfare in the area. Descent is patrilineal and residence is patrilocal to maximize the cohesion of the local group as a warriorhood. Hamlets are composed of tiny exogamous patriclans that facilitate marriage within the group and exchange with other hamlets, again based on the local politics of warfare. Traditionally, all marriage was arranged; courtship is unknown, and social relationships between the sexes are not only ritually polarized but also often hostile. Like other Highlands societies of New Guinea, these groups are associated with a men's secret society that ideologically disparages women as dangerous creatures who can pollute men and deplete them of their masculine substance. The means of creating and maintaining the village-based secret society is primarily through the ritual initiation of boys beginning at ages seven through ten and continuing until their arranged and consummated marriages, many years later. The warriorhood is guaranteed by collective ritual initiations connecting neighboring hamlets. Within a hamlet, this warriorhood is locally identified with the men's clubhouse, wherein all initiated bachelors reside. Married men frequent the clubhouse constantly; and on occasion (during fight times, rituals, or their wives' menstrual periods) they sleep there. An account of Sambia culture and society has been published elsewhere and need not be repeated here (Herdt 1981).

Sambia sexual culture, which operates on the basis of a strongly essentializing model of sexual development, also incorporates many ideas of social support and cultural creation of the sexual; these ideas derive from the role of ritual and supporting structures of gendered ontologies throughout the life course of men and women. Sexual development, according to the cultural ideals of the Sambia life plan, is fundamentally distinct for men and women. Biological femaleness is considered "naturally" competent and innately complete; maleness, in contrast, is considered more problematic since males are believed incapable of achieving adult reproductive manliness without ritual treatment. Girls are born with female genitalia, a birth canal, a womb, and, behind that, a functional menstrual-blood organ, or *tingu*. Feminine behaviors such as gardening and mothering are thought to be by-products of women's natural *tingu* functioning. As the *tingu* and womb become engorged with blood, puberty and menarche occur; the menses regularly follow, and they are linked with women's child-bearing capacities. According to the canonical male view, all women then need is a penis (i.e., semen) in facilitating adult procreation by bestowing breast milk (transformed from semen), which prepares a woman for nursing her newborn. According to the women's point of view, however, women are biologically competent and can produce their own breast milk—a point of conflict between the two gendered ontologies. This gives rise to a notion that women have a greater internal resilience and health than males and an almost inexhaustible sexual appetite. By comparison, males are not competent biologically until they achieve manhood, and thus they require constant interventions of ritual to facilitate maturation.

The Sambia believe that boys will not "naturally" achieve adult competence without the interventions of ritual, an idea that may seem strange but is actually common throughout New Guinea, even in societies that do not practice boy-inseminating rites (Herdt 1993). Among the Sambia, the practice of age-structured homoerotic relations is a transition into adulthood. The insemination of boys ideally ends when a man marries and fathers a child. In fact, the vast majority of males—more than 90 percent—terminate their sexual relations with boys at that time. Almost all the men do so because of the taboos and, to a lesser degree, because they have "matured" to a new level of having exclusive sexual access to one or more wives, with genital sexual pleasure being conceived of as a greater privilege.

The sexual culture of the Sambia men instills definite and customary lifeways that involves a formula for the life course. Once initiated (before age ten), the boys undergo ordeals to have their "female" traces (left over from birth and from living with their mothers) removed; these ordeals involve painful rites, such as nose-bleedings, that are intended to promote masculinity and aggression. The boys are then in a ritually "clean" state that enables the treatment of their bodies and minds in new ways. These boys are regarded as "pure" sexual virgins, which is important for their insemination. The men believe that the boys are unspoiled because they have not been exposed to the sexual pollution of women, which the men greatly fear. It is thus through oral intercourse that the men receive a special kind of pleasure, unfettered by pollution, and the boys are thought to acquire semen for growth, becoming strong and fertile. All the younger males are thus inseminated by older bachelors, who were once themselves semen recipients.

The younger initiates are semen recipients until their third-stage "puberty" ceremony, around age fifteen. Afterward, they become semen donors to the younger boys. According to the men's sacred lore and the dogmas of their secret society, the bachelors are "married" to the younger recipient males—as symbolized by secret ritual flutes, made of bamboo and believed to be empowered by female spirits that are said to be hostile to women. During this time, the older adolescents are "bisexuals" who may inseminate their wives orally, in addition to the secret insemination of the boys. Eventually these youths have marriages arranged for them. After they become new fathers, they in turn stop sexual relations with boys. The men's family duties would be compromised by boy relations, the Sambia men say.

The growth of males is believed to be slower and more difficult than that of females. Men say that boys lack an endogenous means for creating manliness. Males do possess a *tingu* (menstrual blood) organ, but it is believed to be "dry" and nonfunctional. They reiterate that a mother's womb, menstrual blood, and vaginal fluids—all containing pollution—impede masculine growth for the boy until he is separated by initiation from mother and the women's world. Males also possess a semen organ (*keriku-keriku*), but unlike the female menstrual blood organ, it is intrinsically small, hard, and empty, containing no semen of its own. Although semen is believed to be the spark of human life and, moreover, the sole precipitant of biological maleness (strong bones and muscles and, later, male secondary-sex traits: a flat abdomen, a hairy body, a mature glans penis), the Sambia hold that the human body cannot naturally produce semen; it must be externally introduced. The purpose of ritual insemination through fellatio is to fill up the *keriku-keriku* (which then stores semen for adult use) and thereby masculinize the boy's body as well as his phallus. Biological maleness is therefore distinct from the mere possession of male genitalia, and only repeated inseminations begun at an early age and regularly continued for years confer the reproductive competence that culminates in sexual development and manliness.

There are four functions of semen exchange: (1) the cultural purpose of "growing" boys through insemination, which is thought to substitute for mother's milk; (2) the "masculinizing" of boys' bodies, again through insemination, but also through ritual ordeals meant to prepare them for warrior life; (3) the provision of "sexual play" or pleasure for the older youths, who have no other sexual outlet prior to marriage; and (4) the transmission of semen and soul substance from one generation of clansmen to the next, which is vital for spiritual and ritual power to achieve its rightful ends (Herdt 1984b). These elements of institutionalized boy-inseminating practices are the object of the most vital and secret ritual teachings in first-stage initiation, which occurs before puberty. The novices are expected to be orally inseminated during the rituals and to continue the practice on a regular basis for years to come. The semen transactions are, however, rigidly structured homoerotically: Novices may act only as fellators in private sexual interactions with older bachelors, who are typically seen as dominant and in control of the same-sex contacts. The adolescent youth is the erotically active party during fellatio, for his erection and ejaculation are necessary for intercourse, and a boy's oral insemination is the socially prescribed outcome of the encounter. Boys must never reverse roles with the older partners or take younger partners before the proper ritual initiations. The violation of such rules is a moral wrong that is sanctioned by a variety of punishments. Boy-inseminating, then, is a matter of sexual relations between unrelated kin and must be seen in the same light as the semen exchanges of delayed sister exchange marriage: Hamlets of potential enemies exchange women and participate in semen exchange of boys, which is necessary for the production of children and the maturation of new warriors.

Ritual initiation for boys is conducted every three or four years for a whole group of boys as an age-set from neighboring villages. This event lasts several months and consists of many ordeals and transitions, some of them frightening and unpleasant, but overall welcomed as the entry into honorable masculinity and access to social power. It culminates in the boys' entry into the men's clubhouse, which is forbidden to women and children. The boys change their identities and roles and live on their own away from their parents until they are grown up and married. The men's house thus becomes their permanent dormitory and secret place of gender segregation.

Sambia girls do not experience initiation until many years later, when they undergo a formal marriage ceremony. Based on what is known, it seems doubtful that the girls undergo a sexual period of same-gender relations like those of the boys, but I cannot be sure because I was not permitted to enter the menstrual hut, where the initiations of girls were conducted. Males begin their ritual careers and the change in their sexual lives early because the transformation expected of the boys is so great. Girls live on with their parents until they are married and achieve their first menstruation, which occurs very late, age nineteen on average for the Sambia and their neighbors. A secret initiation is performed for the girls in the menstrual hut. Only then can they begin to have sexual relations with their husbands and live with them in a new house built by husband and wife.

The first-stage initiation ceremonies begin the events of life crisis and change in identities for the boys. They are young. After a period of time they are removed to the forest, where the most critical rituals begin to introduce them to the secrets of the men's house and the secret society of the men's warriorhood. The key events involve bloodletting rituals and penis-and-flute rites, which we study here from observations of the initiation conducted in 1975 (Herdt 1982). Here the boys experience the revelation of sexuality and the basic elements of their transition into age-structured homoerotic relations.

On the first morning of the secret rituals in the forest, the boys have fierce and painful nosebleeding rituals performed on them. This is believed to remove the pollution of their mothers and the women's world that is identified with the boys' bodies. But it is also a testing ground to see how brave they are and the degree to which their fathers, older brothers, and the war leaders of the village can rely on the boys not to run and hide in times of war. Afterward, the boys are prepared by their ritual guardian, who is referred to as their "mother's brother," a kind of "male mother," for the main secret teaching that is to follow. They are dressed in the finest warrior decorations, which they have earned the right to wear through the initiation ordeals. And this begins their preparation for the rites of insemination that will follow. Now that their insides have been "cleansed" to receive the magical gift of manhood—semen—they are taken into the sacred chamber of a forest setting, and there they see for the first time the magical flutes, believed to be animated by the female spirit of the flute, which protects the men and the secrecy of the clubhouse and is thought to be hostile to women.

The key ceremony here is the penis-and-flutes ritual. It focuses on a secret teaching about boy insemination and is regarded by the men and boys alike as the most dramatic and awesome of all Sambia rituals. It begins with the older bachelors, the youths with whom the boys will engage in sexual relations later, who enter the chamber dressed up as the "female spirits of the flutes." The flute players appear, and in their presence, to the accompaniment of the wailing flutes, some powerful secrets of the men's cult are revealed. The setting is awesome: a great crowd waiting in silence as the mysterious sounds are first revealed; boys obediently lining up for threatening review by elders; and boys being told that secret fellatio exists and being taught how to engage in it. Throughout the ritual boys hear at close range the flute sounds associated since childhood with collective masculine power and mystery and pride. The flutes are unequivocally treated as phallic—as symbols of the penis and the power of men to openly flaunt their sexuality. The intent of the flutes' revelation is threatening to the boys as they begin to guess its meaning.

I have observed this flute ceremony during two different initiations, and although my western experience differs greatly from that of Sambia, one thing was intuitively striking to me: The men were revealing the *homoerotic meanings* of the sexual culture. This includes a great preoccupation with the penis and with semen but also with the mouth of the boy and penile erection, sexual impulses, homoerotic activities in particular, and the commencement of sexuality in its broadest sense for the boys. If there is a homoerotic core to the secret society of the Sambia, then this is surely where it begins. These revelations come as boys are enjoined to become fellators, made the sharers of ritual secrets, and threatened with death if they tell women or children what they have learned. They have to keep the secret forever.

Over the course of many years I collected the stories of the boys' experiences as they went through these rituals. The boys' comments indicated that they perceived several different social values bound up with the expression of homoerotic instruction in the flute ceremony. A good place to begin is with childhood training regarding shame about one's genitals. Here is Kambo, a boy who was initiated, talking about his own experience: "I thought—not good that they [elders] are lying or just playing a trick. That's [the penis] not for eating. . . . When I was a child our fathers said, 'This [penis] is not for handling; if you hold it you'll become lazy.' And because of that [at first in the cult house] I felt—it's not for sucking." Childhood experience is a contributing source of shame about fellatio: Children are taught to avoid handling their own genitals. In a wider sense Kambo's remark pertains to the taboo on masturbation, the sexual naïveté of children, and the boys' prior lack of knowledge about their fathers' homosexual activities.

Another key ritual story concerns the nutritive and "growth" values of semen. A primary source of this idea is men's ritual equation of semen with mother's breast milk, as noted before. The initiates take up this idea quickly in their own subjective orientations toward fellatio. (Pandanus nuts, like coconut, are regarded as another equivalent of semen.) The following remark by Moondi is a typical example of such semen identifications in the teachings of the flute ceremony: "The 'juice' of the pandanus nuts, . . . it's the same as the 'water' of a man, the same as a man's 'juice' [semen]. And I like to eat a lot of it [because it can give me more water], . . . for the milk of women is also the same as the milk of men. Milk [breast milk] is for when she carries a child—it belongs to the infant who drinks it." The association between semen and the infant's breast food is also explicit in this observation by Gaimbako, a second-stage initiate: "Semen is the same kind as that [breast milk] of women. . . . It's the very same kind as theirs, . . . the same as pandanus nuts too. . . . But when milk [semen] falls into my mouth [during fellatio], I think it's the milk of women." So the boys are taught beliefs that are highly motivating in support of same-gender sexual relations.

But the ritual also creates in boys a new awareness about their subordination to the older men. Kambo related this thought as his immediate response to the penis teaching of the flute ceremony: "I was afraid of penis. It's the same as mine—why should I eat it? It's the same kind; [our penises are] only one kind. We're men, not *different* kinds." This supposition is fundamental and implied in many boys' understandings. Kambo felt that males are of one kind, that is, "one sex," as distinct from females. This implies tacit recognition of the sameness of men, which ironically suggests that they should be not sexually involved but in competition for the other gender. Remember, too, the coercive character of the setting: The men's attempt to have boys suck the flutes is laden with overt hostility, much stronger than the latent hostility expressed in lewd homosexual jokes made during the preceding body decoration. The boys are placed in a sexually subordinate position, a fact that is symbolically communicated in the idiom that the novices are "married" to the flutes. (Novices suck the small flute, which resembles the mature glans penis, the men say.) The men thus place the boys in an invidious state of subordination during which the boys may sense that they are being treated too much like women. Sometimes this makes them panic and creates fear and shame. In time, however, a different feeling about the practice sets in.

Nearly all the novices perform their first act of fellatio during the days of initiation, and their story helps us to understand what happens later in their masculine development. Let me cite several responses of Moondi to this highly emotional act:

> I was wondering what they [elders] were going to do to us. And . . . I felt afraid. What will they do to us next? But they put the bamboo in and out of the mouth; and I wondered, what are they doing? Then, when they tried out our mouths, I began to understand . . . that they were talking about the penis. Oh, that little bamboo is the penis of the men. . . . My whole body was afraid, completely afraid, . . . and I was heavy, I wanted to cry.
>
> At that point my thoughts went back to how I used to think it was the *aatmwogwambu* [flute spirit], but then I knew that the men did it [made the sounds]. And . . . I felt a little better, for before [I thought that] the aatmwogwambu would get me. But now I saw that they [the men] did it.
>
> They told us the penis story. . . . Then I thought a lot, as my thoughts raced quickly. I was afraid—not good that the men "shoot"

me [penetrate my mouth] and break my neck. Aye! Why should they put that [penis] inside our mouths! It's not a good thing. They all hide it [the penis] inside their grass skirts, and it's got lots of hair too!

"You must listen well," the elders said. "You all won't grow by yourselves; if you sleep with the men you'll become a *strong* man." They said that; I was afraid. . . . And then they told us clearly: semen is inside—and when you hold a man's penis, you must put it inside your mouth—he can give you semen. . . . It's the same as your mother's breast milk.

"This is no lie!" the men said. "You can't go tell the children, your sisters." . . . And then later I tried it [fellatio], and I thought: Oh, they told us about *aamoonaalyi* [breast milk; Moondi means semen]—it [semen] is in there.

Despite great social pressures, some boys evince a low interest in the practice from the start, and they seldom participate in fellatio. Some novices feverishly join in. Those are the extremes. The great majority of Sambia boys regularly engage in fellatio for years as constrained by taboo. Homoerotic activities are a touchy subject among males for many reasons. These activities begin with ceremony, it is true, but their occurrence and meaning fan out to embrace a whole secret way of life. What matters is that the boys become sharers of this hidden tradition; and we should expect them to acquire powerful feelings about bachelors, fellatio, semen, and the whole male sexual culture.

One story must stand for many in the way that the Sambia boys grow into this sexual lifeway. One day, while I was talking idly with Kambo, he mentioned singing to himself as he walked in the forest. I asked him what he sang about; and from this innocuous departure point, he said this: "When I think of men's name songs then I sing them: that of a bachelor who is sweet on me; a man of another line or my own line. When I sing the song of a creek in the forest I am happy about that place. . . . Or some man who sleeps with me— when he goes elsewhere, I sing his song. I think of that man who gave me a lot of semen; later, I must sleep with him. I feel like this: he gave me a lot of water [semen]. . . . Later, I will have a lot of water like him."

Here we see established in Kambo's thought the male emphasis on "accumulating semen" and the powerful homoerotic relationships that accompany it. Even a simple activity like singing can create a mood of subjective association with past fellatio and same-gender relationships with the older males. Kambo's last sentence contains a wish: that he will acquire abundant manliness, like that of the friend of whom he sings.

No issue in recent reviews has inspired more debate than the basic question of whether—or to what extent—sexual feelings and erotic desires are motives or consequences of these cultural practices. Does the Sambia boy desire sexual intercourse with the older male? Is the older male sexually attracted to the boy? Indeed, what does "erotic" or "sexual" mean in this context, and is "desire" the proper concept with which to gauge the ontology? Or do other factors, such as power or kinship, produce the sexual attraction and excitement (conscious or unconscious) necessary to produce arousal and uphold the tradition (Herdt 1991b)?

Although Sambia culture requires that men eventually change their focus to marriage and give up boy-inseminating, some of the men continue to practice age-structured relations because they find them so pleasurable. A small number of individual men enjoy inseminating boys too much to give up the practice. They develop favorites among the boys and even resort to payment of meat when they find it difficult to obtain a boy who will service them. In our culture these men would probably be called homosexuals because of their preference for the boys, their desires, and their need to mask their activities within the secret domain of ritual. But such an identity of homosexual or gay does not exist for the Sambia, and we must be careful not to project these meanings onto them, for that would be ethnocentric. We can, however, see how they live and what it means to have such an experience—in the absence of the sexual identity system of western culture.

One of these men, Kalutwo, has been interviewed by me over a long period of time, and his sexual and social history reveals a pattern of broken, childless marriages and an exclusive attraction to boys. As he got older, he would have to "pay" the boys with gifts to engage in sex, but when he was younger, some of the boys were known to be fond of him as well (Herdt and Stoller 1990). Several other males are different from Kalutwo in liking boys but also liking women and being successfully married with children. They would be called bisexual in our society. They seem to enjoy sexual pleasure with women and take pride in making babies through their wives, yet they continue illicitly to enjoy oral sex with boys. But Kalutwo disliked women sexually and generally preferred the closeness, sexual intimacy, and emotional security of young men and boys. As he got older, it was increasingly difficult for him to obtain boys as sexual partners, and this seemed to make him feel depressed. Moreover, as he got older, he was increasingly at odds with his male peers socially and stood out from the crowd, having no wife or children, as expected of customary adult manhood. Some people made fun of him behind his back; so did some of the boys. In a society that had a homosexual role, Kalutwo might have found more social support or comfort and perhaps might have been able to make a different transition into middle age. But his village still accepts him, and he has not been turned away or destroyed—as might have occurred in another time had he lived in a western country.

Perhaps in these cases we begin to understand the culture of male camaraderie and emotional intimacy that created such deeply felt desire for same-gender relations in ancient Greece and Japan, in which sexual pleasures and social intimacies with the same gender were as prized as those of intercourse and family life with women. No difficulty was posed to society or to self-esteem so long as these men met their social and sexual obligations and were honorable in their relations with younger males. We know from the anthropological reports from New Guinea that such individuals existed elsewhere as well, and among the Malekula and Marind-anim tribes, for example, adult married men would continue such relations with boys even after reaching the age of being grandfathers in the group, for this was expected.

Mojave Two-Spirit Initiation

My reading of the gender-transformed role among American Indians has shown the importance of two spirits in Native American society for the broader understanding of alternative sexualities. What I have not established thus far is the development of the role in the life of the individual. Among the Mojave Indians, a special ceremony in late childhood marked a transition into the third-gender role that allowed for homoerotic relations so long as they were between people in different gender roles. The two spirit was the product of a long cultural history that involved myth and ceremonial initiation. The ceremonies were sacred and of such importance that their official charter was established in the origin myths of the tribe, known from time immemorial. The meanings of this transition deserve to be highlighted as another variation on coming of age ceremonies in nonwestern cultures.

The Mojave child was only about ten years old when he participated in the ceremony for determining whether a change to two spirit would occur. Perhaps this seems young for a coming of age ceremony; but it might be that the very degree of change and the special nature of the desires to become a man-woman required a childhood transition. In the Mojave case, it was said that a Mojave boy could act "strangely" at the time, turning away from male tasks and refusing the toys of his own sex. The parents would view this as a sign of personal and gender change. Recall that mothers had dreams that their sons would grow up to become two spirits. No doubt this spiritual sign helped to lend religious support for the ceremony. At any rate these signs of gender change were said by the Mojave to express the "true" intentions of the child to change into a man-woman. Nahwera, a Mojave elder, stated: "When there is a desire in a child's heart to become a transvestite that child will act different. It will let people become aware of that desire" (Devereux 1937, 503). Clearly, the child was beginning to act on desires that transgressed his role and required an adjustment, through ritual, to a new kind of being and social status in the culture.

Arrangements for the ceremony were made by the parents. The boy was reported to have been "surprised" by being offered "female apparel," whereon the relatives waited nervously to see his response. Devereux reported that this was considered both an initiation and an ultimate test of the child's true desires. "If he submitted to it, he was considered a genuine homosexual. . . . If the boy acted in the expected fashion during the ceremony he was considered an initiated homosexual, if not, the gathering scattered, much to the relief of the boy's family" (Devereux 1937, 508). The story suggests that the parents in general may have been ambivalent about this change and may not have wanted it. Nevertheless, true to Mojave culture, they accepted the actions of the boy and supported his decision to become a two-spirit person. The Mojave thus allowed a special combination of a child's ontological being and the support of the family to find its symbolic expression in a ready-made institutionalized cultural practice. It only awaited the right individual and circumstances for the two-spirit person to emerge in each community in each generation.

Both the Sambia example of age-structured relations and the Mojave illustration of gender-transformed homosexuality reveal transitions in late childhood up to age ten. What is magical about age ten? It may be that certain critical developmental changes begin to occur around this time—desires and attractions that indicate the first real sexuality and growing sense of becoming a sexual person. In fact, our study in Chicago revealed that nine and one-half years for boys and ten years for girls were the average age when they were first attracted to the same gender (Herdt and Boxer 1996).

Coming Out—Gay and Lesbian Teens in America

Ours is a culture that defines male and female as absolutely different and then goes to great lengths to deny having done so; American culture reckons "heterosexual" and "homosexual" as fundamentally distinctive kinds of "human nature" but then struggles to find a place for both. Although such gender dimorphism is common in the thinking of nonwestern peoples, the latter idea is rare in, even absent from, many cultures—including our own cultural ancestors, the ancient Greeks. The Greeks described people's sexual behaviors but not their being as homosexual or heterosexual. As we have seen, the Greeks did not place people in categories of sexuality or create sexual classifications that erased all other cultural and personality traits. In our society today this kind of thinking is common and permeates the great symbolic types that define personal being and social action in most spheres of our lives. For many heterosexuals, their worldview and life course goals remain focused on the greatest ritual of reproduction: the church-ordained marriage. And this leads to parenting and family formation. Many think of this ritual process as "good" in all of its aspects. Others see same-gender desire as an attack on that reproductive and moral order, a kind of crisis of gender and sexuality that requires the assertion of a mythical "family values," descended from nineteenth-century ideals, that are seldom relevant to heterosexuals today, let alone to gays and lesbians.

Coming out is another form of ritual that intensifies change in a young person's sexual identity development and social being. It gives public expression to desires long felt to be basic to the person's sexual nature but formerly hidden because of social taboos and homophobia. The process leads to many events that reach a peak in the person's young adult years, especially in the development of gay or lesbian selves, roles, and social relations. Coming out continues to unfold across the entire course of life: There is never really an end to the process for the simple reason that as gay or lesbian people age and their social situations change, they continue to express in new, relevant ways what it means to be gay or lesbian. Such a social and existential crisis of identity—acted out on the stage of the lesbian and gay community—links the social drama of American youths' experiences with those of tribal initiations, such as those of the Sambia and Mojave, played out in the traditional communities. Of course, these two kinds of drama are different and should not be confused, but they share the issues of handling same-gender desires in cultural context.

Two different processes are involved. First is the secretive act of "passing" as heterosexual, involving the lone individual in largely hidden social networks and secret social spaces. We saw the effects of this secret life in the history of homosexuality in Chapter 2. In many towns and cities, especially unsophisticated and traditionally conservative areas of the country, the possibilities are only now emerging for gay/lesbian identification and social action. Second is the coming out in adolescence or young adulthood.

Initially the gay or lesbian grows up with the assumption of being heterosexual. As an awareness of same-gender desires emerges, a feeling of having to hide these desires and pretend otherwise, of acting straight, leads to many moments of secrecy. Later, however, sexual and social experiences may yield a divergent awareness and a desire to be open. What follows is a process of coming out—typically begun in urban centers, sometimes in high school, sometimes later, after the young person has left home for college, work, or the service—that leads to self-identification as gay or lesbian. Through these ritual steps of disclosure all kinds of new socialization and opportunities emerge, including entrance into the gay and lesbian community.

Being and doing gay life are provisioned by the rituals of coming out, and they open significant questions for thinking about youths in search of positive same-gender roles. American teenagers may seem less exotic to the gay or lesbian reader; but they are more of an oddity to the heterosexual adult community as they come out. To many in our own society, these youths look "queer" and "strange" and "diseased," attitudes that reflect historical stereotypes and cultural homophobia.

The growing visibility of the lesbian and gay movement in the United States has made it increasingly possible for people to disclose their desires and "come out" at younger ages. Over the past quarter century, the evidence suggests that the average age of the declaration of same-gender desires has gotten earlier—a lot earlier, as much as ten years earlier than it was in the 1970s—and is for the first time in history a matter of adolescent development. It is not a matter for everyone, of course, but increasingly for those who become aware and are lucky to have the opportunities to begin a new life. In our study of gay and lesbian self-identified youths in Chicago, we found that the average age for boys and girls' "coming out" was sixteen. But we also found that the earliest awareness of same-gender attraction begins at about age ten, which suggests that the desires are a part of the deeper being of the gay or lesbian person.

Gay and lesbian teenagers are growing up with all of the usual problems of our society, including the political, economic, and social troubles of our country, as well as the sexual and social awakening that typifies the adolescent experience. I have already noted how American society and western cultures in general have changed in the direction of more positive regard for gays. This does not mean, however, that the hatred and homophobia of the past are gone or that the secrecy and fear of passing have faded away. People still fear, and rightly so, the effects of coming out on their lives and safety, their well-being and jobs, their social standing and community prestige. These youths are opting to come out as openly lesbian or gay earlier in the life course than ever before in our society. Yet they experience the troubles of feeling themselves attracted to the same gender, with its taboos and sorrows of stigma and shame, not knowing what to do about it. Fortunately, the gay and lesbian culture provides new contexts of support; these youths have institutions and media that talk about it; they learn from adult role models that they can live relatively happy and rewarding lives with their desires.

We can study how one group of adolescents in Chicago has struggled with these issues while preparing for socialization and coming out in the context of the lesbian and gay community. The study of gay, lesbian, and bisexual youths in Chicago was located in the largest gay social services agency of the city, Horizons Community Services. Horizons was created in the early 1970s out of the gay liberation movement, and by 1979 it had founded a gay and lesbian youth group, one of the first in the United States. The agency is based in the gay neighborhood of the city, and it depends on volunteers and the goodwill and interest of friends of the agency. In recent years the youths have lead the Gay and Lesbian Pride Day Parade in Chicago and have become a symbol of social and political progress in gay culture in the city.

The Horizons study was organized around the youth group, for ages thirteen to twenty, but the average age of the youths interviewed in depth was about eighteen. We interviewed a total of 202 male and female youths of all backgrounds from the suburbs and inner city, white and black and brown. Many people of color and of diverse ethnic subcultures in Chicago have experienced racism and many forms of homophobia, and these have effectively barred their coming out. The group tries to find a place for all of these diverse adolescents; no one is turned away. Group meetings are coordinated by lesbian and gay adults, esteemed role models of the teens. They facilitate a discussion of a variety of topics, particularly in matters of the coming out process, such as fears and homophobic problems at school or home, and issues of special interest to the teens. The youth group has an active social life as well, hosting parties and organizing social events, such as the annual alternative gay and lesbian prom, held on the weekend of high school proms in Chicago, for the youth members.

Protecting teens from the risk of infection from AIDS is another key goal of Horizons' sponsorship of the youth group. AIDS has become an increasingly important element of the youth group discussions. "Safe sex" is promoted through educational material and special public speakers. In general, the socialization rituals of the group prepare the youths for their new status in the gay and lesbian community, and the rituals culminate in marching in the Gay and Lesbian Pride Day Parade every June.

The lesbian or gay youth is in the throes of moving through the symbolic "death" of the heterosexual identity and role and into the "rebirth" of their social being as gay. As a life crisis and a passage between the past and future, the person is betwixt and between normal social states, that is, between the heterosexual worlds of parents and the cultural system of gay and lesbian adults. To the anthropologist, the youths are symbolically exiting what was once called "homosexuality" and entering what is now called "gay and lesbian." To the psychologist, their transition is from dependence and internalized homophobia to a more open and mature competence and pride in the sexual/gender domains of their lives. The transformative power contained in the rituals of coming out as facilitated by Horizons helps in the newfound development of the person. But it also helps in the lives of everyone touched by a youth who is coming out. As long as this process is blocked or resisted, the pull back into passing as heterosexual is very tempting.

Back in the 1960s, as we have seen from the account of Evelyn Hooker's work (Chapter 2), coming out was a secret incorporation into the closet "homosexual" community. Studies at the time showed that the more visible contexts of engaging in same-sex contacts might lead to de facto coming out, but these were generally marginal and dangerous places, such as public toilets, where victimization and violence could occur. To come out in secret bars, the military, toilets, or bus depots did not create a positive identification with the category of gay/lesbian. There was generally no identity that positively accorded with gay or lesbian self-esteem as we think of it today. Thus, we can understand how many people found it revolutionary to fight back against homophobia and begin to march openly in parades in the 1970s. Nevertheless, the change was uneven and difficult.

People who continue to pass as straight when they desire people of the same gender and may in fact have sexual relations with them present a perplexing issue—not only for lesbians and gay men but also for society as a whole. This kind of person, through secrecy and passing, serves as a negative role model of what not to be. Alas, there are many movie stars, celebrities, and sports heroes who live closeted lives of this kind—until they are discovered or "outed" by someone. Many youths are frightened or intimidated when they discover adults they know and love, such as teachers, uncles, family friends, or pastors, who pass as heterosexual but have been discovered to desire the same gender. Adolescents can be angered to discover that a media person they admire has two lives, one publicly heterosexual and one privately homosexual. This is a cultural survival of the nineteenth-century system of closet homosexuality, with its hide-and-seek games to escape the very real dangers of homophobia. In contrast, positive role models provided by the largely white middle-class adult advisers at Horizons are the crucial source for learning how to enter the gay and lesbian community.

Cultural homophobia in high school is a powerful force against coming out. Learning to hide one's desires is crucial for the survival of some youths, especially at home and at school, the two greatest institutions that perpetuate homophobia in the United States. Our informants tell us that standard slurs to put people down in the schools remain intact. To be slurred as a "dyke" or a "faggot" is a real blow to social esteem. But "queer" is the most troubling epithet of all. To be targeted as a "queer" in high school is enormously troubling for the youths, somehow more alienating and isolating, an accusation not just of doing something "different" but of being something "unnatural." One seventeen-year-old eleventh grade boy remarked to us that he was secretive at school. "I'm hidden mostly—cause of the ways they'll treat you. Okay, there are lots of gangs. . . . They find out you're [what they call] a faggot and they beat on you and stuff. If they ask me I say it's none of their business." The role of secrecy, passing, and hiding continues the homophobia. Ironically, as Michelle Fine (1988, 36) notes in her study of black adolescent girls in New York City high schools, it was the gay and lesbian organization in the school that was the most open and safe environment in which young African-American girls could access their own feelings. They could, with the support of the lesbian and gay teenage group, start to become the agents of their *own* desires. Our study has shown that in Chicago most lesbian or gay youths have experienced harassment in school; and when this is combined with harassment and problems at home, it signals a serious mental health risk, especially for suicide. And the risk of suicide before lesbian or gay youths come to find the support of the Horizons group is very great.

The ritual of coming out means giving up the secrecy of the closet. This is a positive step toward mental health, for life in the closet involves not only a lot of hiding but also a good deal of magical thinking, which may be detrimental to the person's well-being. By magical thinking, I mean mainly contagious beliefs about homosexuality such as the common folk ideas of our culture that stereotype homosexuality as a disease that spreads, as well as the historical images of homosexuality as a mental illness or a crime against nature. These magical beliefs support homophobia and warn about the dangers of going to a gay community organization, whispering how the adolescent might turn into a monster or sex fiend or be raped or murdered or sold into slavery.

Another common contagious fear is the belief that by merely contacting other gays, the adolescent's "sin or disease" will spread to the self and will then unwittingly spread to others, such as friends and siblings. One of the common magical beliefs of many adults and parents is that the youth has merely to avoid other gay and lesbians in order to "go straight." This is surely another cultural "leftover" from the dark myth of homosexuality as evil, discussed in Chapter 2. If the adolescent will only associate with straights, the parent feels, this strange period of "confusion" will pass, and he or she will become heterosexual like everyone else. Such silly stereotypes are strongly associated with the false notion that all gay or lesbian teens are simply "confused," which was promoted by psychologists in the prior generation. This belief is based on the cultural myth that same-sex desires are "adolescent" desires of a transient nature that may be acquired or learned but can go away; and if the self ignores them, the desire for the opposite sex will grow in their place. Magical fears of contracting AIDS is a new and most powerful deterrent to coming out among some youths. Many youths fear their initial social contact with anyone gay because they think they might contagiously contract AIDS by being gay or lesbian or by interacting socially with gays.

The gender difference in the experience of coming out as a male or a female highlights the cultural pressures that are still exerted on teens to conform to the norm of heterosexuality in our society. Girls typically have more heterosexual experience in their histories, with two-thirds of the girls having had significant heterosexual contact before they came to Horizons. Since the age of our sample was about eighteen, it is easy to see that relatively early on, between the ages of thirteen and seventeen, girls were being inducted into sexual relations with boys. We face here the problem of what is socially necessary and what is preferred. Only one-third of the boys had had heterosexual experience, and fully two-fifths of them had had no sexual experience with girls. Note also that for many of the boys, their sexual contacts with girls were their lesbian-identified friends at the Horizons youth group. The boys tended to achieve sexual experiences earlier than the girls, by age sixteen, at which point the differences in development had evened out. Both genders were beginning to live openly lesbian or gay lives.

Clearly, powerful gender role pressures are exerted on girls to conform to the wishes of parents, siblings, peers, and boyfriends. Some of this, to use a phrase by Nancy Chodorow (1992) about heterosexuality as a compromise formation, results in a compromise of their desires, even of their personal integrity, in the development of their sexual and self-concept. But as we know from the work of Michele Fine (1992), who studied adolescent sexuality among African-American girls in the New York City schools, females were not able to explore and express their desires until they located a safe space that enabled them to think out loud. In fact, they could not become the agents of their own desires until they had located the gay and lesbian youth group in the high school! There, some of them had to admit, contrary to their stereotypes, they found the gay youths more accepting and open of variations than any of their peers or the adults. The lesson here is that when a cultural space is created, people can explore their own desires and better achieve their own identities and sociosexual goals in life.

We have found that four powerful magical beliefs exist in the implicit learning of homophobia and self-hatred among gay and lesbian youths. First is the idea that homosexuals are crazy and heterosexuals are sane. Unlearning this idea involves giving up the assumption of heterosexual normalcy in favor of positive attitudes and role models. Second is the idea that the problem with same-gender desires is in the self, not in society. Unlearning this belief means recognizing cultural homophobia and discovering that the problem with hatred lies not in the self but in society. Third is the magical belief that to have same-gender desires means giving up gendered roles as they were previously known and acting as a gender-transformed person, a boy acting or dressing as a girl, a girl living as a boy, or either living as an androgyne. There is nothing wrong with these transformations. What we have seen in the cross-cultural study, however, is that there are a variety of ways to organize same-gender desires. The old ways of gender inversion from the nineteenth century are only one of these. Unlearning gender reversal means accepting one's own gendered desires and enactments of roles, whatever these are, rather than living up to social standards—either in the gay or straight community.

Fourth is the belief that if one is going to be gay, there are necessary goals, rules, roles, and political and social beliefs that must be performed or expressed. This idea goes against the grain of American expressive individualism, in which we feel that each one of us is unique and entitled to "know thyself" as the means of social fulfillment. The key is that there is not one perfect way to be gay; there are many divergent ways. Nor is there any single event, or magic pill, that will enable the process of coming out. It is a lifelong process, as long as it takes to live and find a fulfilling social and spiritual lifeway in our culture.

Lesbian and gay youths have shown that coming out is a powerful means of confronting the unjust, false, wrongful social faces and values of prejudice in our culture. Before being out, youths are asking, "What can we be?" or "How can we fit into this society?" Emerging from the secrecy, these youths are making new claims on society to live up to its own standards of justice. The rituals of coming out are a way of unlearning and creating new learning about living with same-gender desires and creating a positive set of relationships around them. Surely the lesson of the gay movement is that hiding desires and passing as something other than what one is are no less injurious to the normal heart and the healthy mind of gay youths than was, say, passing as a Christian if one was a Jew in Nazi Germany or passing as white in the old South or in South Africa under apartheid.

Lesbian and gay youths are challenging society in ways that are no less revolutionary than discriminations based on skin color, gender, or religion. A new of kind of social and political activism has arisen; it goes beyond AIDS/HIV, but builds on the grief and anger that the entire generation feels about the impact of the pandemic on gay and lesbian culture. Some call this new generation queer. But others prefer lesbian or gay or bisexual or transgendered. Perhaps the word is less important than the commitment to building a rich and meaningful social world in which all people, including lesbians and gays, have a place to live and plan for the future.

We have seen in this chapter how a new generation of lesbian- and gay-identified youths has utilized transition rituals to find a place in the gay and lesbian community. It was the activism and social progress of the lesbian and gay culture that made this huge transformation possible. The emergence of a community enabled the support of youth groups and other institutions for the creation of a new positive role model and self-concept. Youths are beginning to take up new status rights and duties, having a new set of cultural ideas to create the moral voice of being gay, bisexual, lesbian, or queer. The rituals, such as the annual Gay and Lesbian Pride Day Parade, make these newly created traditions a lived reality; they codify and socialize gay and lesbian ideals, knowledge, and social roles, bonding past and future in a timeless present that will enable these youths to find a place in a better society.

◄ 5 ►

Sexual Lifeways and Homosexuality in Developing Countries

IN A VARIETY OF THIRD WORLD countries in which socioeconomic development is rapidly altering the structure of cultural life, people are confronted with new sexual lifeways that challenge political authority, religion, traditional gender roles, and social and familial hierarchies. How are same-gender sexual relations being handled amid revolutionary change? Where previously the sexual culture was represented by the categories man and woman, and sometimes a third sex or gender as well, new categories of gay and lesbian appear on the scene. All too often these newer sexual identities, accompanied by "subcultures" or "sexual networks," give the appearance of being the direct product of transplanted gay/lesbian identity systems from western culture, but such an appearance is more often than not an illusion. The precolonial or preliterate culture has not been dislodged but may be disrupted, with more room at the table for emergent identities. But these have not replaced the traditional categories. Indeed, there are places, such as Thailand, where the emergent lifeways may in certain respects actually give a boost to more traditional third-gender categories that were previously marginalized or not fully incorporated into the emerging state system (Jackson 1995).

There is a strong tendency in current discussions to look on these processes of modernization as if they had begun last week, or last year, or in the last decade, when in fact processes of modernization are centuries old, as we have observed in this book. To anthropologists who are working in civilizations, large and small, old and new, there is a sense in which history is being "made up" before our eyes. This is the allure of globalization—the notion that all of the past has been disrupted; that previous identities, customs, and lifeways are being shuffled off to one side; that a new social production is being prepared for the stage of society. It is for this reason that I purposively begin this chapter with a historical example from nineteenth-century China that links us to the past (as reviewed in Chapter 3).

The new and emergent sexual identity processes can move a people beyond the period of colonialism or encapsulation and into the world system. Some people initially feared globalization because they thought that a hegemonic superstructure would erase all cultural differences and replace all local culture and knowledge. Sexual lifeways were of concern here—a part of the cultural furniture of the past that might be put up for sale or simply junked. In fact, however, this fear now seems exaggerated, as evidenced by the persistence of local tradition, customs, and lifeways. This persistence suggests that even the forces of large-scale globalization have not eroded the tendency of human cultures to incorporate and make things over in their own image as systems of local meanings and homely structures of cultural lifeways.

Historical China

Women have engaged in a variety of role-specialized forms of homosexuality, and one of the most important of these comes from historical China. As we saw in Chapter 3 , for centuries China had a form of man/boy relations and a counterpart for women and girls. (Homosexuality in the modern period has been condemned in China, and lesbianism in particular seems to be regarded as scandalous

[Hinsch 1990; Sankar 1986].) A more complex and historically specific form of role-organized same-gender relations emerged out of the economic conditions of nineteenth-century factory life for women in southern China. This was one of the earliest documented examples of how "development" and colonization affected local sexual cultures and transformed what was a role-specialized homosexuality into a new paradigm for modernization.

Under the influence of the encroachment of western powers such as Germany and England and the waning power of the Ching dynasty, great change began to overtake China. New industrial enterprises appeared, among them increasingly large silk factories in the Pearl River delta near Canton. These factories took to hiring large numbers of women workers, sent by their families to earn income for struggling parents. These women were particularly well suited for fine silk making and were thus in a strange and privileged position. They vowed not to marry in order to devote themselves to making silk, and they formed strong systems of "sisterhood," which at first involved social solidarity and social, emotional, and financial security. In these conditions a special social role of being unmarried and closely bonded to the sisterhood emerged for women to express their same-gender love and sexual feelings. What began with emotional and physical intimacy seems in some cases to have turned into sexual and romantic love.

This was remarkable in a patriarchal society that disliked lesbianism. These female factory workers and their "marriage resistance movement" became well known throughout the country, which punished lesbianism, and newspaper accounts spoke of this "shameful" development, which between 1865 and 1935 involved as many as one hundred thousand women. Yet these women did their jobs, brought wealth, and were otherwise needed by Chinese society. Some young Chinese women who lived and worked together in silk factories formed erotic and economic bonds with each other. They did not marry and have children, and some of them apparently stayed with their women partners for years. Before the silk industry collapsed and political upheaval occurred, some of these women escaped to other countries, notably Hong Kong.

Dakar, Senegal

As we know from the prior discussion on Africa, reports on the cultural forms of same-gender relations on the African continent are generally scarce. Nevertheless, recent research on same-gender relations in Senegal by Dutch anthropologist Niels Teunis (1996) has demonstrated the existence of an emergent form of role-specialized homoerotic relations. It depends to a significant extent on gender distinctions of the form we saw in Chapter 3. And yet the nature of social control and the modernizing processes associated with a bar in Dakar are reminiscent of similar forms in many parts of the world.

A group of secretive homosexuals in Dakar, the capital city, frequently come together in a marginal bar in the old city. The social environment in Dakar is very hostile toward homosexuals, so the men who meet in that bar make sure that nobody knows they go there. Their sexuality is hidden from their families. The tavern, a place to entertain the tabooed, is also frequented by women who come to drink and smoke and for that reason are called prostitutes, even though most of them are not. The most prominent customers, however, are the homosexuals, a fact whispered throughout the city. This is a closet homosexual bar in the sense known in the past in large cities or still known in smaller towns in western society. The Dakar males have more money to spend and are better fed and dressed than most of the others and take up the rear half of the place.

The Dakar men who come seeking same-gender relations are not exclusively organized by age or gender but are inclined to pair off in active/passive roles that mirror gender hierarchy. Although these homosexuals are called *gordjiguène,* which is the Wolof-language term for "man-woman," there are two kinds of man-woman. Each takes on a different role in sexual intercourse, which typically involves anal intercourse. The men who insert during intercourse are called the *yauss* (penetrators), and the men who receive are called the *oubi* (receivers). A homosexual in Dakar is either a *yauss* or an *oubi.* He does not switch roles during sexual contact or with different partners. Therefore, when a *yauss* desires another man, he will look for an *oubi,* and vice versa.

When these two men come together and have sex, the *yauss* gives some money to the *oubi*. This is typically what happens when a Senegalese man and woman come together. The man gives money to the woman, or he gives her gifts to indicate that the relationship could become more serious and that he might propose to her. Homosexuals do not marry, but they share the same gender dynamic as far as the relationship between the two is concerned. Some of the *oubi* indeed act very effeminate, but most do not. Behaving effeminately in public would expose them as homosexual, and they might suffer dire consequences.

The silence about homosexuality in Africa is unfortunate for several reasons. One is that AIDS prevention efforts in Africa have totally ignored the possibility of HIV transmission in contact between men. Prevention workers simply accept the idea that this form of sexual contact is too infrequent to be of importance. They forget that negative attitudes, which they themselves reflect, make it extremely hard for anyone to discover how men enjoy sex with other men in Africa.

Mexico

The culture of Mexicans, including that of the mestizo, highly values and prizes manliness. The culture sharply contrasts male and female roles, and the exaggerated emphasis on being male and showing courage, aggression, power, and sexual control is known as machismo (from macho, a male animal, a he-goat, a robust, vigorous male). The complex of these qualities and the traditional homosexuality of Mexico are best known from the work of anthropologist Joseph Carrier (1995). He has shown that within Mexican society there are qualities of both the age-structured system of traditional homosexuality and the gender-organized relationships of homosexuality.

However, in recent years the gay and lesbian movement has made some inroads, and a new concept, of the *internacional*, has emerged to indicate someone who plays all parts (passive and active) and might be thought of as an "international" in the sense of homosexual, gay, and lesbian identities and roles. There are also nascent coming out groups in such places as Guadalajara and Mexico City. And much recent work and activism have focused on fighting AIDS and the spread of HIV in Mexico and its neighboring states. For these reasons we must consider Mexico within the context of the larger world system and of those rapidly developing nations that combine old forms and new sexual lifeways.

Traditional Mexican culture has a marked sexual and gender dichotomy. The values of upholding machismo are very strong throughout the society. A powerful symbolic divide exists between "good women" and "bad women," resulting in the prizing of virginity and the consequent postponement of male/female sexual relations. This in turn results in a high percentage of the male population that is unmarried and without sexual resort, which enhances the presence of same-gender relations in the culture. Homosexuality in general is negative and sanctioned within certain circumstances within Mexico. The range of terms applied to it include *maricón*, which is polite and means "sissy," and *puto* and *jot*, which mean "whore" and are vulgar epithets. Stigma is great enough that many homosexuals go to considerable lengths to hide their desires and relations from their families. Closet homosexuality in the nineteenth-century mold fits well with this form of cultural system.

Yet Mexican culture in the barrio is generally supportive of same-gender relations within certain parameters. The person in traditional contexts must conform to the roles and parts that are provided for the partners, taking either the *activo* (active) or *passivo* (passive) roles. A man is never dishonored if he has taken the *activo* role with a younger male or with a transvestite male. The younger male need not be dishonored either if certain precautions are taken. However, to be anally penetrated in Mexico, as in many Latin countries, is the supreme transgression, an act of challenge and defilement and a mode of dishonor that must be defended against. The younger, more feminine acting male may become an object or a target of older males, who may press for sexual service or favors. They may be protective within the neighborhood, but their absolute support cannot be counted on because of the homophobia and machismo of the masculine identity system.

The strong emphasis on male/female dualism lends itself to the presence of transvestite roles and practices among lower-class Mexican males who engage in same-gender relations. According to Norwegian ethnographer Annick Prieur (1994), males who dress as transvestites are typically from the lower classes, and they operate within a system of having to emphasize women's sexual traits, such as breasts and buttocks, makeup and gowns. The perfect body, they feel, is a status symbol, for it shows how hard they have worked and saved to present an image of a "classy and beautiful" transvestite. They face even more difficulty in managing the tension between sexuality and violence.

Being an object of attraction to macho men, the transvestites also risk dishonoring them and arousing their violence. It is the very femininity of the *passivo* homosexuals that makes them attractive to certain heterosexual men, or *mayates*, a term that means macho-looking males who like to have sex with effeminate males. In a curious turn of the tables, it is the effeminate *passivos* who actually pay the macho *mayates* by way of food, drinks, clothes, and other forms of exchange. Their young macho partners often delude themselves by insisting that they are only having the sex "for money" or engaging in same-gender relations because they are "hard up" and "in need of sex." If they are mocked or provoked, the machos may feel shame and become violent. But some of these men seem to prefer same-gender sex to sex with their girlfriends or other females. This suggests the very complicated relations that ensue in a culture that heavily formalizes male/female relations and ritualizes sexuality itself.

The effects of machismo can be seen throughout Latin America. Nicaragua, which went through a civil war and an upheaval that resulted in the establishment of a socialist regime, provides an interesting basis for comparison with Mexico. While the revolutionary government uplifted the conditions of women and mitigated against aspects of machismo, it also took an ambivalent but generally positive attitude toward *cocones*, passive and more feminine males who like same-gender sexual relations. But many of the (heterosexual) revolutionaries came to fear that all men would turn into "queers" (Lancaster 1995). Apparently, in trying to change their macho roles, Nicaraguan men felt threatened by the greater equality of their women, which they felt made them "soft" or effeminate like *co-cones*. As the examples of Nicaragua and Mexico seem to indicate, there is no easy solution to the incorporation of masculine and homosexual roles in times of dramatic and sudden change in sexuality and gender roles. Likewise, Cuba under the Castro regime reveals the many hardships of homosexuals under a repressive government that imprisons them and effectively institutionalizes homophobia, with disastrous effects for the treatment of people with AIDS (Lumsden 1996, 68–69ff).

Brazil

Brazil is a country with a striking range of sexual cultures and a public presence of homosexuality. Yet homosexuality is a relatively recent category for identification, and much of the relevant imagery and language surrounding same-gender desire has been imported from abroad, both from Europe (through the Portuguese colonial history of Brazil) and the United States (through the large number of tourists who come to visit the cities and Carnaval, as well as AIDS campaigns that have drawn on models and ideas from North America). The folk model of sexuality among Brazilians thus builds on a variety of notions that help us to understand the meaning of same-gender desire.

The large country of Brazil is marked by gender and sexual roles that permit a somewhat greater latitude of sexual conduct than European and North American societies. Patriarchy is ideally represented in the power of men, the violence used to sanction roles, the relatively greater sexual freedom of men, and the sexual domination of women. The presence of double standards for men and women and sons and daughters is very noticeable both in social and in moral terms. The history of sexuality in Brazil combines both a colonial history and a reaction to colonial authorities and local Indian customs. In very general terms penis and more general phallic representations emphasize the active sexual agency of the male, and the qualities of the penis are compared to tools and weapons. Brazilian men compare the vagina to the more passive qualities of a receptacle, a mouth, and stress the negative connotations of menstruation as a sickness and a malevolent power. In general, the concept of a queer, of a *bicha* (worm, parasite, female animal), is contrasted with that of a macho, thereby creating binarisms: macho and queer, man and woman, virgin and whore. Anthropologist Richard Parker (1991) has stressed the dynamic nature of and change in homosexuality in Brazil.

Of particular relevance is the widely occurring distinction between active and passive, known locally in Portuguese as *actividade* (masculine, active, penetrator) and *passividade* (feminine, passive, penetrated). There is little conscious reflection on these terms in popular culture such that language and culture could combine in identity and sexual action in new and creative ways. While growing up, boys commonly engage in same-sex games, such as *troca-troca*, in which boys take turns placing their penis in each other's anus. The boys who consistently take the role of feminine recipient seem to become recognized, to become effeminate, and they suffer stereotypes and fortunes similar to those of women in Brazil.

The power of the system suggests that entry into same-gender relations is not in itself sufficient to cause problems for someone, lower his status, or get him into trouble—this part is different from European systems. However, there is a condition: In male/male relations the man does not sacrifice his masculinity so long as he plays the active role, the *actividade*, just as we have seen in Mexico and other gender-role-stratified groups. But the male partner who takes the passive role jeopardizes his masculinity by upsetting the hierarchy of gender roles. The latter may make himself into a *bicha*.

Alongside these changes, the AIDS epidemic has had an impact on Brazil and the gay and lesbian community that we are only now beginning to understand because of the large and diverse nature of the population and the difficulty of measuring the disease. We do know that a high proportion of Brazilians, both heterosexual and homosexual, engages in anal sex, as revealed by household survey studies. Reasons for this might include the use of the anus as an alternate orifice for sex to avoid pregnancy and the pleasure and excitement associated with anal sex. Brazilians have an idea of sexual excitement that flirts with what is tabooed, hidden, and dangerous, and anal sex falls within this transgressive category. Tradition and sexual excitement are thus of a piece: the inside and outside of bodily experience and sexual relations in society. What can at one historical time be the very essence of decorum can in other times become the most titillating and lewd of aesthetics.

Brazil is a society in which this theme of transgressive sexual excitement created out of what is forbidden seems intensely marked. What "occurs behind closed doors" and what is tempting but illicit are at the very core of sexuality in Brazil. "The penetration of a prick in an ass-hole is really known as dirty sex, not just because it's the asshole that defecates. . . . It's the conception of social structure. This type of incorporation of filth is placed in all the meanings of things that are done outside of the taboos of society" (Parker 1991, 119). Sexual transgression in Brazil is a moral crime, and the sinner is a criminal. What defines the difference between these cultural ideas are the fantasies and excitement of the particular actor; but these form trends and trajectories within a culture by virtue of the shared life plans and sexual lifeways of a people.

In recent years new concepts and identities—homosexual, heterosexual, and bisexual—have come to Brazil. A small but growing homosexual liberation movement has been visible since the 1970s. A gay movement, or *comunidade gay,* has emerged around the concept of gay identity (*identidade gay*). These new forms apparently grew out of elite and middle-class knowledge and power in Brazil, but with a definite influence from Europeans and Americans. Now Brazil has the largest and most dynamic gay culture outside of the entire set of western cultures. Yet this culture is not just an imitation of the West. The old ideas of passive/active and so on are being placed into the movement and take shape in eclectic forms. For example, a concept of *entendid*—meaning "one who knows" or "understands," implying knowledge but also agency—has come into conversation. It implies a new model of being, of defining sexual relations through a preference for sex only with those who are homosexual or gay identified. This model suggest a change in the overall organization of sexual culture and lifeways in Brazil. This has important implications for sexual desire as a negotiated meaning system that draws attention to difference, diversity, and the ever-changing contexts of homosexuality in Brazil.

India

India is a country of immense cultural diversity and many sexual cultures. Its hierarchical social system, supported by religious castes and highly gender-polarized relationships between men and women, provides the backdrop for one of the most significant examples of a third sex in the world. The Hijra is a special caste of ascetics whose members are devoted to worship of the Mother Goddess and whose cult has the ritual power of blessing births and weddings in India. The Hijras come almost exclusively from poor backgrounds and ideally renounce material things in favor of devotion and asceticism. They are typically biologically normal men and some hermaphrodites all of whom elect to be castrated in order to join the caste and serve the Goddess. Their sacred role also has an undercurrent of power and fear because they are capable of cursing people who fail to give them alms when they beg and of causing infertility and impotence in those who might see their deformed genitals. The Hijras might be defined as being neither male nor female, or the sacred "female man" of northern India, and thus as being a third sex created by the castration ceremony. The transformation of this role in the context of modernization in India is of great import for the cross-cultural study of emerging sexual cultures.

The Hijras are known from the writings of scholars dating back to at least the eighteenth century, but today they are best described in the work of anthropologist Serena Nanda (1990). The Hijras are typically biologically normal men who feel a kind of calling to transform their sex into females and must then be castrated to become authentic members of the caste for the rest of their lives. As children they do not seem exceptional. However, a few are born as hermaphrodites, and any of these are claimed by the Hijras as their "natural children," who are then taken into the caste. They are blessed by the Mother Goddess and seek protection from Her in their ritual and mythological traditions. Even though they are somewhat of an embarrassment to Indian Hindu society, they are also utilized for their ritual functions. They are known to be well organized in certain towns and cities, following a guru and living as an extended family.

Once a person has felt the desire to become a Hijra and has been castrated, he will retire for a period of forty days following castration in a ritual seclusion that mirrors the birth and liminal period of a mother after childbirth in India. Castration is done in secret, being illegal by Indian law, and is performed by a kind of Hijra midwife. It is a dangerous operation, and the life of the castrate is in the balance for some time. But the process finally yields powers of regeneration and creative asceticism as defined by sexual abstinence and ritual practices and prayer. The Hijra's sense of being called to this life may provoke a desire for confirming omens, although we cannot be entirely sure of the motivations leading a person to become a Hijra. After she has healed, she will dress up as a woman and wear the kinds of clothes, jewelry, makeup, and hairstyles that are her right as a Hijra man-woman.

The sexual life of the Hijras is complicated by the fact that they are strongly associated with the ascetic traditions of Shiva and Hinduism. They are communicants of the divine power of the Mother Goddess, which makes them transformers—the impotence they experience as men being changed into the creative and ritual powers of the instruments of the Mata, the Mother Goddess. Therefore, ideally the Hijras should not engage in sexual relations. Many do so, however, and in the contemporary scene they may even serve as commercial sex workers. Many Hijras report that as adolescents they engaged in same-gender sexual relations. They feel that by having had passive sex and serving as the anal recipient of other men, they were "spoiled" for heterosexual relations with women. Some Hijras also experience love and romance in their relations. They may find a good deal of fulfillment in their lives, especially their later lives, not unlike that of Indian women. They may also move into the role of being a leader, or guru, of the clan, which brings generative power to transmit the traditions to future generations.

There are no female Hijras, of course, but there are women known to dress as men in northern India. Unmarried celibate females who dress and act as men in many contexts in the Kangra fringe area of the Himalayas have been known for centuries. Although the Hijras are the result of castration, whereas the Indian women who dress as men are rare and created from gender-role distinctions only, the two sacred variations on male/female are significant for an understanding of how same-gender desires might be organized in one of the world's oldest and largest civilizations.

Today the spread of AIDS in India is a matter of great concern, both in the general heterosexual population and among male sex workers and Hijras who engage in receptive anal intercourse. Efforts on the part of health workers and the World Health Organization to inform and highlight education and prevention of the spread of disease help to further understanding of the behavior of the Hijras. Through the collection of individual life histories and sexual surveys, health workers have discovered that a much larger number of males are engaging in same-gender relations than was previously known in Indian society. This knowledge has in turn shown the importance both of studying what actually occurs in people's real-life situations and keeping a perspective on the ideals of their culture, which may hide what is actually occurring "on the ground." Where once the Hijras were ritual performers, today a variety of social pressures are leading them into commercial sex and prostitution. The emergence of competing groups, including the nascent gay and lesbian movement, is significant here. Younger Indians coming of age today are placed in the awkward situation of feeling that they may be classified as Hijras if they enter into open same-gender erotic relations. Gays and Hijras mix in a complicated way that will surely lead to further rapid change in the local system of sexual classification and lifeways.

Kathoey of Thailand

Thailand is a country known for its open sexuality. Indeed, Longman's 1993 *Dictionary of the English Language* describes Bangkok, the capital city, as a country known for prostitution. Thailand has a thriving sex industry, built on sex clubs, prostitution, massage parlors, and a variety of erotic and pornographic literature and media. In fact, in traditional times female prostitution was rather common in Thailand and was not particularly disparaged as in the West. A woman might engage in prostitution but later be married and have children without noticeable stigma. The great majority of Thai men of all ages regularly visited prostitutes in villages and towns, attesting to prostitution's historical place in the sexual culture of arranged marriages in Thailand. Homosexuality has been long known in the country and is generally more accepted than in many other cultures. Thailand is increasingly known for the visibility of homosexuality and a particular kind of third gender, *kathoey*.

Australian scholar Peter Jackson (1995) has written an interesting book that details many of the letters written by Thai homosexuals to a famous magazine columnist, Go Pak-nam, or "Uncle Go" (a fictitious name). Uncle Go stresses the importance of anal sex and often advises his correspondents to accept their same-gender desires and try to be happy with them. These letters are filled with romance and heartbreak stories of men who fall in love with men, are involved with married men, are worried about sex "through the back door" (a favorite metaphor for anal sex in Thailand). Such material demonstrates not only that same-gender desires occur among the Thai people and may be given voice in this way, but also that Thai homosexuals are recognized enough as a group that the most influential magazine in the country serves as a vehicle for the expression of their desires and complaints.

Thailand is a patriarchal country whose modern history is characterized by the fact that it remained free of colonization, having successfully outmaneuvered the British and other European powers in prior centuries. Consequently, Thailand has a proud history, and this quality is to be found in the warmth and self-confidence of the Thai people. The main background influence on marriage, male/female relations, and homosexuality is Buddhism. It takes a generally positive and supportive view of sexuality, as I noted in the discussion of Japan. Buddhism is also mildly positive about homosexuality, though monks themselves are supposed to refrain from sexual relations of all kinds, and unlike the Japanese tradition noted earlier, this injunction in contemporary life seems apparent.

Little is known of Thai female sexuality and homosexuality in particular. But the dualism of male/female, masculine/feminine is marked in the culture. Woman is defined as an object of male desire, and the fetishization of women here, through makeup, sexual surgery to enhance the nose and breasts, and the great popularity of beauty contests of all kinds—including contests of drag and *kathoey* in transvestite clothes—is a significant sign of Thai male attitudes. Most recently homosexuality as a formal category has come to Thailand, and the country has witnessed the birth of a new gay and lesbian movement, brought on in part by the incursion of western tourism and in part by the AIDS epidemic, both of which have heightened awareness of same-gender desire and its meaning.

Though sexuality is approved in Thailand, the situation for homosexuals is far from perfect, and social pressure is exerted on many to pass as heterosexual. Male homosexuals who stand out from the crowd may be stigmatized for it, whereas female homosexuals are already subordinated to men within Thai culture, no matter what they do. In general, however, both gays and lesbians are lumped together in local conversations that refer to the "homosexual problem" (*panha rak-ruam-phet*).

The category *kathoey*, or third gender, is a biological male who dresses and acts as a woman but takes some pride in his male genitals. *Kathoey* have some basis in the mythology and ancient lore of Thailand, being mentioned in critical texts that suggest the very old and lasting importance of this figure in Thai culture. Many *kathoey* have such a feminine appearance that they easily pass as biological females and remain undetected by others unless they self-identify or become sexually aggressive. Being a part of the sex industry in many quarters, *kathoey* behave and dress in moderately to largely dramatic and exaggerated ways, with loud and abrasive language and aggressive overtures—uncharacteristic of the Thai people in general and women in particular, who are soft-spoken and may be shy in public interaction. *Kathoey* is a kind of mediator of male/female relations, influencing sexuality, romance, passion, and spirituality in all relationships.

Whereas in history the concept of *kathoey* referred to same-gender behavior in this special role, in modern times it is increasingly used as an identity for homosexuality, albeit negative, in the sense of faggot. *Kathoey* in certain situations are subject to attack and sexual assault, including rape. Yet they are more visible than transvestites or transsexuals in western countries. Some of them have ordinary jobs, whereas others work in prostitution. The success and popularity of *kathoey* are suggested by the recent BBC documentary *Lady Boys,* which tells the story of two *kathoey* in the 1990s as these teens begin their careers as a third gender.

Globalization, Gay/Lesbian Identities, and AIDS

Homosexuality is not being imported wholesale into developing countries, not even by sexual tourism, as is sometimes asserted in the media. But neither are traditional sexual cultures and lifeways immune to the imprint of gay and lesbian roles from the western world. Local sexual cultures can easily appropriate some of the meanings of "gay and lesbian" as concepts, which are then tacked onto far more complex and rich lifeways as if they were identical. We are not dealing here with simple questions of a traditional culture changing into a complex one, of old wine in new bottles, as Margaret Mead might once have said of the rapid social change in the Pacific that resulted from World War II. Nor is the traditional or precolonial cultural system of the local group so easily discarded in favor of the importation of the identity system of gay and lesbian. Even when the identity is used, the cultural context is not imported along with it. To use gay and lesbian portable identity markers and signs in Bangkok and Mexico City and Rio de Janeiro is not the same as doing so in Boston and London and Paris, no matter how sophisticated and western in appearance those great capitals of the Third World seem to a western tourist.

To re-create the totality of an identity system of gay and lesbian signs requires both the cultural context and the identity markers, and that re-creation is seldom achieved, except in the most "Americanized" or "western" gay bars and clubs of the developing world, designed to create the cultural illusion of the familiar in the strange. Things are more complicated than such a scenario implies, for the forces of history, economy, and politics play their roles in the transformations of cultures and sexual lifeways. In the modernizing states, however, we have to consider the sea change in which the former modes of organization of same-gender relations (discussed in Chapter 3)—age, gender, and role organizations of homosexuality—might give way to or be strongly changed by entrance into the world system.

As those changes occur, sexuality is increasingly seen from the perspective of identity rather than from the point of view of traditional social practices and roles. This shift derives in part from the influence of the western identity concepts of gay, lesbian, and bisexual and in part from the effect of the pandemic of AIDS/HIV, which has focused on individuals and to certain uniform public health messages and media around the world. In this transformation we should also consider how the western classification system of identities and roles has been exported elsewhere, through tourists, media, and popular culture, to create a new fabric of individualistic sexual lifeways. Global contact and communication—the sense of an emerging lesbian and gay social network around the world—can be seen in many of the great capitals, East and West. Mass air transportation has enabled people to visit all corners of this shrinking globe toward this end.

But we must not think that the whole of local culture and its modes of thinking about same-gender relations has changed. Instead, new themes and identities are brought in, but at the level of everyday life much remains to be added to these identities from local meanings and practices.

Throughout the world studies have demonstrated how sexual risk for HIV can be transmitted through anal, oral, and coital sex with infected partners. The rate of spread of HIV is slowing down in western countries but speeding up in developing ones. We have seen some examples of this in prior sections. Culture and society are of vast importance in the formation of sexuality, but whatever change has occurred with the transition to modernity, it seems likely that the AIDS epidemic is even more portentous of future social and sexual change, especially in developing nations.

The cultural representation of AIDS has made the public more aware of homosexuality in many countries, but unfortunately often in negative ways. The same is true of the developing countries, with their emerging identities of gay and lesbian. In the United States, from the first homophobic depiction of AIDS as a "gay disease," with the moral victimization implied by such a metaphor, up to the present time, in which HIV is a significant and growing threat to heterosexuals in most areas, the thinking about AIDS has changed.

AIDS has ironically brought gay culture and solidarity more into the minds of gay and lesbian people every day. It was through campaigns within the gay and lesbian community to protect its own, educate itself about safer sex, organize to take care of the sick, and lobby for more government action to support persons with AIDS that the main work was done. The same is true elsewhere.

The risk to gays and lesbians in all cultures stems from the perpetuation of fear and hatred of all kinds. But the risk also comes from homophobia and the presence of cultural values that encourage violence and hatred toward gays, lesbians, and other persons who engage in sexual relations with the same gender. We have seen a great range of cultures and their modes of handling the issues of homosexuality. Among these has been the degree to which the society tolerates variation and supports sexual and gender diversity. For a young person to come out and be more open is a huge step, and it goes more smoothly with the support of the adult world and the society. The range of benefits and resources that enable their coming out is impressive, even from the perspective of world cultures. Increasingly, gays and lesbians stand out as a progressive force for socialization in western society, which seems intimidated by change. Let us hope that positive trends increase in the future, enabling a swift end to the epidemic and progress in society toward building on the lessons so hard learned from the epidemic.

◀ 6 ▶

Lesbians, Gays, and Bisexuals in Contemporary Society

NOW THAT WE HAVE REACHED the end of this study of other cultures, we can reflect on what we have learned and its relevance for gays and lesbians closer to home. Let us see what new perspectives we can bring to an understanding of sexual culture and lifeways in the United States, especially the development of what we might call a new sexual culture and community of gay men and lesbians in America. We also need to touch on the rapidly changing meanings of bisexuality. And the implications of AIDS as reviewed in this study also deserve a final mention.

Today understandings of sexual variations and alternative lifeways cannot be divorced from the larger study of cultural diversity and multiculturalism. We have seen that there are many similarities and many differences in the concepts and roles of gays and lesbians across cultures. Whether we emphasize the former or the latter depends on our perspectives, politics, and social aims. And cultural diversity in the United States is forever complicated by the fact that this is perhaps the most socially and ethnically complex nation yet known on this planet. Much of gay and lesbian life is now specific to its cultural scenes and institutions; even its language is gay-defined in some places (Leap 1996).

Multiculturalism in this context means having respect for the different languages and cultural traditions that fill out a sexual culture. These lifeways bring meaningfulness, grace, and beauty to a people, the kind of dignity and historical identity that enables them to feel part of a larger whole, whether it is a civilization or a state. Sexual cultures, including the communities of western culture and the emerging spaces and places in developing nations, must be seen in this light. As the emerging American lesbian and gay culture gains increasing acceptance, those who identify with its institutions as social practices, such as the Annual Gay and Lesbian Pride Day Parade, desire to join as full citizens who expect their social rights and duties to be granted them as openly gay or lesbian. This in turn creates reactions from fundamentalists and moralists who deny the existence of such a sexual culture.

Cultural diversity in the United States thus requires acceptance of alternative sexual lifeways—a difficult but entirely necessary step in the tradition of a liberal democracy that claims that the individual liberties of its citizens are of most importance (Herdt and Boxer 1996). This is a lesson of even greater importance at this point in our history as a society, when notions of diversity are increasingly criticized and under attack, especially by those who have grown uneasy with the alternative lifeways that differ from their own ideals or "family values" as these actually existed or were imagined to have existed in the mythic past (Weeks 1985).

The variety of sexual relationships between persons of the same gender in the United States is immense and subject to all the factors that form sexual cultures in all other times and places. Where age, gender, social roles, social class, and special institutions and social practices play a larger part in other historical societies, in the United States these have been subsumed into a larger ideal pattern of "egalitarianism." When I say that the other forms, such as age-structured homosexuality, have been subsumed, I do not mean "replaced" since we can find examples of virtually all the other forms in this country. Rather, American society has focused acute attention on the emergence of equality and democracy in sexual and gender relationships across the board. Thus, it is no surprise that in the area of homoerotic relations, egalitarian-structured relationships are also emphasized and, within the context of the gay and lesbian movement over the past few decades, also idealized as the preferred form of social and sexual partnership.

We are witness to historical changes of unprecedented magnitude in the acceptance of same-gender relations around the world. Of course, there is much progress to be made, and terrible instances of homophobia and violence are daily directed at gays and lesbians. But the positive advance of attitudes and laws in recent decades is impressive, and although there are great counterforces on the other side, increasing numbers of people in liberal democracies accept sexual orientation as a basic component of being human and the rights of gays and lesbians as important to justice. Three centuries ago homosexuality was punished by death in most western countries. Only a generation ago violence and punishment, social regulation and ostracism, were so common as to form both the mythology and the reality of being homosexual in our society. Today, however, gays and lesbians are experiencing a growing freedom from oppression, and many hold the view that sexual orientation should be a basic human right to be defended by the courts of the world and championed by such organizations as the United Nations and Amnesty International. It is being celebrated in many cities and towns of the United States in an annual Gay and Lesbian Pride Day Parade.

Such enormous change is hard for many parents and grandparents to comprehend; they have not yet incorporated the revolution in the social rights and understanding of homosexuality that has occurred in many parts of the western world. The U.S. lesbian and gay movement is thus leading the way and providing new ideas for freedom from oppression. Yet in another real sense, our study of nonwestern peoples in prior chapters suggests that the United States is just beginning to "catch up" to the basic tolerance and humanity shown to homosexuals in other cultures for centuries. This is part of the story of this chapter.

From Closet Homosexuality
to Gayness and Lesbianism

Historical study has found that a great transformation in ideas and same-gender practices in the West occurred in the transition from the nineteenth to the twentieth century. After the middle of the last century, a new focus on homosexuality as a negative but unified category of being and knowing—ontology and epistemology—began to make immense progress in science and medicine and society, including the attitudes of the rising middle class. The explicit identity became known as homosexual, marked for males loving males, sometimes known as the "intermediate sex," but generally typified by secrecy and the hiding of sexuality to avoid the punishments of the times. What has now become known as the closet homosexual (Sedgwick 1990) was primarily the bearer of a secret sin, disease, and crime, as we have seen. This dark secret was eloquently captured in Oscar Wilde's classic crypto-ethnography *The Picture of Dorian Gray*. Here a contrast between outer beauty and secret monster suggested the makings of closet homosexuality, which was growing during the time and remains a voice on the margins of society today.

During this same era, a new reform movement began to reshape homosexuality. It was first prominent in Europe, especially Germany and England, but it quickly found voices in the United States. The new emancipation movements of feminism and homophilia were able to effect gradual change in social attitudes. This paved the way for a variety of significant political and legal reforms—in law, in science and health, in psychiatry, in the prison system, and in all manner of attitudes, from how to think about masturbation to acceptance of gender-crossing. Within a generation or so, at least within major cities such as New York, the identity of gay and lesbian in many of its current meanings began to emerge (Chauncey 1994). From this source emancipation became a road to political activism, to a kind of new sexual nationalism: a force against homophobia. The gay and lesbian movement in the United States still stands for these progressive developments.

The sources of this cultural and psychological change bear close examination. Rather than viewing the change as the result of new social practices, we might focus on how sexual identity provided a model and a means of organizing new desires and relationships. As an ideology and a personally internalized system of beliefs and ideas, the sexual identity of homosexuality served as a cultural model for the times, organizing same-gender desires and practices in a manner that may be compared to what we have learned of age, gender, and special roles in nonwestern cultures.

I noted earlier that homosexuality as a definite concept preceded the invention of the concept heterosexuality. That the homosexual was constructed first is perhaps explained by the culture's attention to deviations from the reproductive and dimorphism model. Notice that the concept homosexual was implicitly marked as male, whereas the heterosexual category referred both to male and female. Notice also that the occurrence of nonreproductive acts, acts of sexual pleasure, were marked as the explicit content of inversion, later to be transformed into a highly moralistic diagnosis of "perversion," that is, sexual acts whose pleasure derives from harm to the object. A significant clue for the historical interpretation of third-sex/-gender categories is this: They are morally objectionable because the actors are motivated by cultural realities, including those that depart from normative western male/female roles and that involve pleasure, not reproduction, which violates the dominant ideology and the hierarchy of social status positions on which it is founded. In short, the system of sexual identities created a whole normative system and moral ideals of normal and abnormal, ready for the emerging middle class to live by—and to judge itself and others against.

A change in attitudes about plurality and diversity of sexualities and genders has emerged. In the nineteenth century, the preoccupation with the sexual dimorphism of male and female and the gendered duality of heterosexual and homosexual were everywhere. But things have been changing in this century, again the result of many social, economic, and political forces, such as the entry of women into the economy and the existence of two-income families. Among the structural forces thought to have contributed to this change are the human rights movements, greater sexual equality for women, the shift from an industrial to a service economy, and demographic alterations that created "blended" families. The emphasis on public confessions of same-gender desires, the public performance of the role, and the political resistance and refusal to hide and be secret are constitutive of the new gay and lesbian roles. Another significant dimension of emphasis is on the equality of gay partners, their refusal to take canonical gender roles (such as male/husband and female/wife roles in sexual intercourse), and the ideological notion that equality should reign in relationships.

Now in the late twentieth century these features are being renegotiated through new social forms—the gay and lesbian movement in certain western nations in particular. It is apparent from current social science research that this latter social and psychological category is distinct from the third-sex closet homosexual and should not be confused with it. Indeed, we might suggest that gay/lesbian images mediate the male/female, heterosexual/homosexual dualism of the later modern period in western culture in some powerful ways.

The transition from nineteenth- to twentieth-century identities—from secret to public—found its home in the streets and radical politics of recent times. In the shift from "homosexual" to "gay" we are dealing with a cultural transformation of such large proportions that virtually no part of the developing person's lifeways, selfhood, and existence is left unchanged by the acculturation into the emerging gay and lesbian culture. My study of coming out rituals (discussed in Chapter 4) supported this view. Furthermore, I have noted that coming out is not one event but a lifelong social and developmental change not only in the gay or lesbian person, but also in their families and network of friends and neighbors. Some of these aspects, such as involvement in social and political activism, a search for positive friendships, and love and erotic conceptions, are of great import in the meanings of gay culture today.

Before the end of World War II, the idea of a gay/lesbian sexual culture and community was largely unknown. The importance of the political act of coming out was its opposition to incorporation into the secretive "homosexual" community because the category change from heterosexual to homosexual was stigmatizing and discrediting of personhood. Without institutional support, the pejorative cultural meanings of sexual identity category change reduced the problem to one of category change in individual self-representation. Negative and stigmatized signs of "homosexuality" were not enviable: There were no gay and lesbian movement and no social institutions available to promote positive identifications with the category gay. In the United States, where these issues were strongly polarized, the demise of closet homosexuality was signified by the fierce battle fought to end its medical classification as a disease. After the declassification of homosexuality as a disease by the American Psychiatric Association in 1973, progress increased in several areas, including the expansion of the category of gay/lesbian to include both genders, persons of color, a broader spectrum of socioeconomic classes, and a wider range of ages across the course of life.

Coming out continues to pose an economic threat that is a definite barrier to the emergence of gay and lesbian lives (Murray 1996). In a capitalist society, based as it is on competition in the marketplace, coming out is a potential loss of social capital: Employers and clients fear that because of homophobic reactions, they will lose markets. Gays who come out risk losing their jobs or their income—the result of the diminished social status of the employer or the family and the loss of face or privilege in the community that "homosexuals" unwittingly transfer to their significant others in a homophobic society. Such losses of socioeconomic status and class standing pose a formidable barrier to coming out. One of the key social consequences of this barrier is that in general rich people do not come out—they have the most to lose and the least to gain. Things have not much changed on this score in American society; coming out poses a loss of status and power for upper-class families that form a circle of wealth. How much is materially at risk by coming out—the losses or gains of social status and mobility—thus depends on whether the actor is lower, middle, or upper class, with the negative effects on the opportunity structure relevant not only to the "homosexual" but also to his or her "symbolic capital" in society. Perhaps this explains why so few of the members of the great moneyed American families and the highest-paid celebrities and sports stars have come out or why gay and lesbian political figures and television commentators remain hidden or silent. And there are professions, such as the law, that remain very conservative and homophobic. All of the discrimination and hiding deprives the younger generation of positive role models.

In Chapter 4 we saw how a new pattern of coming out in adolescence is fundamentally changing how we might think about gay and lesbian lives at the end of the twentieth century. This developmental pattern suggests not only that the secrecy of the homosexuality stereotype is coming to an end, but also that the late twentieth century is facilitating the early onset of desires in western countries. The ideas of being a "lesbian mother" and a "gay father" are indicative of these trends. Increasingly, the refusal to be classified as heterosexual or homosexual, or to accept a range of desires and gendered relations, has been focused in the emergence of the category of the "queer." The term implies an active rejection of the stigma and hatred of homosexuality in the past and a playful, liminal, creative exploration of new ontologies and gender relations in society. After all, adolescence in general is saturated with sexual images and stereotypes and rebelliousness in the eyes of many Americans. The new sexual identity politics of the queer is increasingly placed into cultural representations as a sign of change in the imagery of the body, as in the prevalence of body piercing among younger Americans, as much as of the body politic. Attempts to regulate the sexuality of the person and resistance to reproductive heterosexuality, including ambivalence regarding marriage and motherhood among women, are no doubt a part of this important change. Yet the overall relations between the sexes and the growing acceptance of same-gender relations suggest that a new chapter in sexuality and gender is opening up in western nations.

Gay and lesbian represent a novel kind of social difference that challenges the older morality of procreation and the larger point of "symbolic reproduction" of the American culture. It does this largely by suggesting a divergent way of organizing sexuality and gender—some call it "gender blending"—that cuts across the existing categories of American social life. As a utopian social movement with claims to a new political and economic constituency, especially in the large urban centers, gay challenges not only the white middle class but also ethnic constituencies. Americans are perhaps more ambivalent about the concept of "sexual identity" than they are about the new "cultural minorities," such as the "African American" or "Japanese American." The ideal of plural ethnic voices gains currency, but only so long as it serves the mainstream. For instance, some authorities challenge these notions, along with "gay and lesbian" as a minority group, because they believe that the expanding multitude splinters, rather than unites, that swirling mass: "American culture." But a basic problem arises for gays and lesbians, too: If being gay is a part of all cultures, it can never be a culture of its own.

In confronting this idea, we can return to the problems and prospects of living in the United States.

The ideals of our society are contradictory in this respect—one ideal celebrates the diversity and meeting of Old and New World cultures; another emphasizes that all of us will blend together in a melting pot and form a happy family. The melting pot was an illusion, of course, but so perhaps are the utopian aims of gay and lesbians to form a single "community" that represents one and all. As Richard Herrell (1992) has pointed out in his important study of the Gay and Lesbian Pride Day Parade, each ethnic community and/or sexual culture is provided a special time and place to occupy the city geography and symbolize its temporary control of the turf. Indeed, in the general concept of "identity," as, for instance, in the construction African American, gay, or Japanese American, we permit the image of plural ethnic voices, but only so long as these highlight the centripetal society. We recognize at a superficial level ethnic variation, and even commemorate subculture variations, as, for instance, in St. Patrick's Day parades, Cinco de Mayo parades, and Martin Luther King Jr. Day. For many people, gay and lesbian represent a new social difference, a culture, and a form of sexuality and gender that cuts across the existing categories of social life. Some people are opposed to multiculturalism, as, for instance, in the repeated resistance of organizers of the St. Patrick's Day Parade in Boston to permit Irish-American gays and lesbians to walk in the parade. Calls to change and integrate gay and lesbian into the mainstream traditions are utopian. Perhaps as a new form of sexual and gendered culture, gay/lesbian lifeways challenge some of Americans' most basic and cherished assumptions about human nature, such as the need to form a nuclear family and rear children as a heterosexually married couple. Such challenges are breaking down accepted norms of social life—that is, of the social contract between the individual and the society—and introducing new notions of sexual identity, attraction, and love, hence suggesting the basis for a different conception of human nature as the foundation of a new cultural minority.

Gays and lesbians come in all shapes and colors and derive from all classes, castes, religious heritages, and cultures. Because of this immense diversity, many gay activists claim that same-gender desire is a part of each culture, even if this desire is not at home in a particular culture. To see this in larger perspective, I wish to compare the United States to Holland, my second home.

The Netherlands

It is possible for a country to undergo a revolution in its cultural treatment of homosexuality; a case in point is the Netherlands. The category homosexual was preceded in the Netherlands of the golden age (and then in England) by one or another form of the category sodomite. Almost three hundred years ago public opinion held that only the execution of someone who had dared to love another of the same gender would suffice to restore the social and political order (van der Meer 1994). Men who engaged in same-gender sexual relations were called sodomites, and they were compared to a kind of street whore with rouged cheeks and limp wrists. In fact, in this view the sins and disease of the sodomite were so heinous and horrible that they had to be kept secret in Holland. Homosexuals were sometimes tortured, tried, and executed in absolute secrecy until 1730. From that year onward, following the discovery of a secret network of sodomites, executions were then carried out in public to warn others about the "evil." This continued up to 1811, when the Napoleonic Code was introduced. More than one hundred males were executed during this time in Holland, and hundreds more were tried and jailed. Children were convicted of sodomy and were sentenced to life imprisonment. Somewhat later in Germany, sodomy as a social category was expanded to include the bizarre lumping of sexual acts with people of the same sex and sexual acts between Jews and non-Jews on the grounds that a Jew was an animal; and thus it followed that all unnatural, that is, nonreproductive, acts were placed together. But by the later nineteenth century these excesses were gone, and the closet homosexual had emerged in Holland and Europe more widely.

Twentieth-century struggles for emancipation of homosexuals in the Netherlands were given shape by the Dutch Society for Integration of Homosexuality/Center for Culture and Relaxation (NVIH/COC). Founded in 1946, the COC—as it is known today—

began with the name the Shakespeare Club. The club was under close surveillance by the police, and the authorities tried to stop club meetings, but this organization proved to be a big success. Even before the war there existed the Dutch Scientific and Humanitarian Committee (NWHK). Founded in 1911 and organized after the German organization of the same name (created by the famous sexologist Magnus Hirschfeld), the NWHK was devoted to improving the position of homosexual men and women in Dutch society.

The NWHK was a response to Article 248b of the Dutch penal code. That article forbade sexual contact of an adult with a minor of the same sex. A comparable code did not exist for sexual contact between all people of different sexes. The rationale for Article 248b was that homosexuality was something like a communicable disease, and therefore the state had to protect the youth of the country. But throughout the century, more effort was put into harassing homosexual men and women, with this law in hand, than into protecting youth. And so the article was a thorn in the side of homosexuals and thus a spearhead in the struggle for homosexual emancipation. The abolishment of Article 248b in 1971 is for that reason celebrated as a milestone in the struggle for homosexual emancipation in the Netherlands.

The Dutch have not forgotten the lesson of the Nazis and of Adolf Hitler's "final solution" of genocide, in which millions were killed, among them several thousand people suspected of being homosexuals who were rounded up by the fascists and put in prison camps. Gay and lesbian culture has adopted as one of its dominant iconic symbols the "pink triangle" by which these victims of the Nazis were identified. The symbol emerged as an instruction in a historical lesson: The Nazis enforced a naive "naturalist" ideology of reproduction that made men superior to women, abortion a crime against the state, and homosexuality a moral drain and threat to the reproductive virility of the Fatherland.

The Shakespeare Club held its first meeting on December 7, 1946 (the club changed its name in 1949). It was a literary evening, and a famous scholar of the classics gave a lecture on men-boy love in ancient Greece. In this first evening, the character of the Shakespeare Club was evident. The name had been chosen to reflect the club's goal—to be a cultural organization—but also to evoke the homo-erotic desire in some of Shakespeare's sonnets. The content of the evening was also well chosen for its day. In a time of severe Protestant Christianity, many homosexuals feared that they were immoral, sick, or sinful. The Shakespeare Club therefore showed them a wide variety of historical examples of homosexual contact, paying attention to famous literary people whose homosexuality was known, such as Erasmus, André Gide, and Oscar Wilde. The COC not only tried to educate its members; it also tried to educate Dutch society about the moral standards of club members and thereby suggest that homosexual men and women should be perceived as the model citizens many of them were.

During the 1950s, the COC remained a welcome meeting place for homosexuals in a society that was still very hostile toward same-sex preference. The COC's success was such that many chapters of the organization were founded outside of Amsterdam. In Amsterdam two COC bar/dance clubs existed that were highly successful and attracted tourists from the world over. The COC became more of a political organization in 1962. The name changed again, in 1964, to the Dutch Organization for the Integration of Homophiles/Center for Culture and Relaxation. The self-confidence of many homosexuals was visible under this new name since they no longer regarded homosexuality as an individual problem. The NVIH/COC maintained that, rather than homosexuals being the problem, society was the source of the problem.

The main discriminatory piece of legislation had become history. This happened at the brink of a new era of homosexual life; this was the beginning of the transition of a notion of homosexuality to a system of gay and lesbian identity formation. A movement started in which gay men and lesbian women came out of the closet openly to show the world that they were there and that they expected to be accepted on their own terms.

At the same time, many gays and lesbians organized their social life increasingly with other gays and lesbians. Gays and lesbians came together to such an extent that the community became a kind of neighborhood focus, but not as defined in the American concept of a "gay ghetto." In some ways this was an achievement because it represented a legitimate, safe place for lesbians and gays to be together. But some worried about the price to be paid for this kind of community: namely, that Dutch society would condone gays and lesbians only within that "ghetto." It was as if a cordon sanitaire were being constructed around the community, and it was becoming increasingly difficult to cross the border into the larger society, where the existence of gays and lesbians did not have much consequence. These worries notwithstanding, many people with a same-sex preference look with astonishment at the achievement of the gay and lesbian movement and the freedom it celebrates (even if confined to the gay and lesbian community).

Today it is possible for persons of the same gender to exercise their own choice of partner after age sixteen, and in many cases it is possible for those who choose to do so to enter into a marriage contract that is partially accepted by the government of Holland. AIDS activism has energized many gays and lesbians in the country and has become an important political and social activity as well. Many homosexuals would like the state to legalize their partnerships in the same way that heterosexual marriages are accepted and to allow adoption, but this remains a roadblock. Permitting same-gender couples to walk down the street holding hands is not only a dream of most lesbians and gay men but also very close to the reality in Holland.

Across Europe one can find reflections of this same kind of historical transformation. England began with somewhat more tolerant attitudes in the time of the sodomite and sapphist and did away with the criminalization of homosexuality earlier than other European nations, including the Scandinavian countries. Today, however, conservative attitudes seem more reactive than those of Holland; laws against pornography are especially harsh and punitive in England. Sweden is a country in which a somewhat more oppressive period of secretive homosexual clubs before World War II would compare with the United States. After the war, however, gay life in Stockholm surged, with many openly gay saunas and bars and the founding of the Swedish Association for Gay and Lesbian Rights in the center of the city. With the advent of AIDS, however, the government moved swiftly to outlaw many of the gay saunas in a move that eroded morale in the country (Hendriksson and Mansson 1995).

France has followed a course somewhat more like that of England, but since the time of AIDS, a greater openness and activism have overtaken urban centers in France. A similar picture can be found in Germany, where the reunification of the country has led to new strains but also to great opportunities for gays and lesbians to become more open than was possible under the communist regime in the former German Democratic Republic. Sex has become increasingly open as a discourse in Russia since the collapse of the former Soviet Union, which severely oppressed homosexuals and opposed the gay movement. As Europe moves toward greater economic integration in coming years, we will look on with great interest to see how the concerns of lesbians and gays are handled in the twenty-first century.

Bisexuality and Sexual Change in America

A generation ago the famous play *Torchsong Trilogy* depicted for the first time a popular and more positive image of gay men. Ironically, the story centers on the life of a female impersonator—a gay man who successfully performed on stage in a nightclub as a transvestite for many years. The play became an immensely successful Broadway production and years later was made into a Hollywood movie. In the movie, a fascinating flashback occurs that embodies perhaps the strongest assumption and stereotype of the gender development of the gay self.

The movie opens with the hero (Harvey Fierstein, the female impersonator) depicted as a happy five-year-old boy who is dressing in his mother's clothes. He is naively applying her makeup to his own face when his mother blithely stumbles on him. She finds him literally "closeted" in her walk-in wardrobe. A large red smudge of lipstick is smeared across his smiling face, and he greets her with baleful laughter. She responds, at first, with amusement, then puzzlement, and at last a troubled glance. Thus, the film telescopes the adult man's life in the childhood scene. It is not surprising that the hero of the story is a successful female impersonator in a New York club associated with bisexuality. Nor is it surprising that gender reversal presages a story of gay liberation in the 1960s and early 1970s, with a steamy love affair and the sentimental "adoption" of a gay teenage son as part of the later adjustment.

The story, for many patrons in the audience and for many researchers in our society as well, is a "just so" origin story to explain how the world of gay men came to be as it is. Once upon a time the story would have been confused with "gender switching" and bisexuality. But increasingly we recognize the mistake in this lumping together. So-called gender-aberrant, dysfunctional, or nonconformist behavior—boys acting as girls and perhaps wanting to be girls—is at the very heart of an older ideology of homosexuality. But the film is fiction, and gender reversal is but a useful assumptive hypothesis derived from our folk science and Freudian notions of same-sex desire and its development. In fact, these ideals probably never applied to the closet homosexual with anything near the strength or purity that authorities once claimed. And even less do they apply to the experience of self-identified gay boys today. The meaning of such childhood behavior has changed, as has the behavior itself.

The act of coming out has defined the self-consciousness of gay and lesbian life for a quarter of a century. Many of us thought of telling others we were gay as the culminating event of our lives—the end of a whole process. And many psychologists and political activists at the time promoted the same kind of life image. Little did we know then that such was not the end but merely the beginning of a new kind of cultural lifestyle and worldview. A new and more challenging period now lies ahead: the definition of life goals and new developmental norms and identities. Being out is not the real object of being gay; it is the beginning of a process, not its end. We in gay and lesbian culture have had to overemphasize the part that coming out plays in the definition of the self. But the lessons that we are learning from the study of children and adolescents especially, but also the life stories of older men who came out very late in life, is that their sense of self is not dependent on being out, even though they desire the same sex.

Coming out and being out are so critical to the creation of self-perceptions, self-esteems, self-representations, and stable positive self-images that they would normally be thought of as crucial to the sense of self in early childhood development. Most writers on the subject of gay and lesbian development have emphasized singular drives and traits that seek stages of self-expression and fulfillment. They have not seemed to recognize that the content and goals of the self come from particular social and historical settings: namely, culture.

In short, development of the self should be thought of as a process of becoming, rather than as a stage, an end point of norms, or a stable script and role. None of the latter ideas applies to the emerging lesbian or gay self for the simple reason that the culture that defines the consciousness of this self is itself changing dramatically. Indeed, the 1969 events of Stonewall and gay liberation in the United States never anticipated the much more complex world of 1996, and the ensuing twenty-seven years of change suggest that we must refine and redefine what it means to be a gay or lesbian self in today's world.

What, after all, is the purpose of a gay life? Is it the seeking of sexual contact with the same sex and that alone? No, many people would say, activists and quiet citizens alike; it is more than that. Is the purpose to secure love and faith with one's lover or friends? What moral action defines the role of the self following the act of coming out? In part, the question of a gay self concerns the nagging sense that the self in the stories of gay life has not yet found a moral voice. Oh, sure, there are plenty of moral concerns and complaints in this. But a moral sensibility and ethics go beyond the act of coming out.

There remains a widely shared myth, inscribed in television, elementary school books, movies, magazines, folklore, and the common experience of everyday playgrounds and supermarkets, that speaks to this issue. It tells of the happy heterosexual and goes a long way in helping to predict how people will develop in our society. Among the cultural lifeways of this myth, the most important include (1) being attracted only to the opposite sex (never to the same sex); (2) having the ceremony of a church wedding that officially sanctions love, romance, and sexual relations with someone of the opposite sex; (3) having one's own biological children with this partner; (4) living with them the rest of one's life; and (5) living to see and enjoy the children of one's children in later years. In the dream image of this child, he or she is happy, healthy, and "normal."

This is a cultural ideal, of course, a script we learn growing up. It resonates most strongly in family life, in school and peer groups, in television soap operas and Hollywood movies, and in church functions. In the lives of many heterosexuals growing up in our society, such a social myth may be a source of parental guidance, psychological comfort, and social support. For others who are unable to live up to these goals, either because they find themselves attracted to the same sex; prefer not to get married; cannot or choose not to have children; become separated, divorced, or widowed; or do not have grandchildren, the myth of the happy heterosexual may be experienced with conflict or as a burden.

The problem of many youths today is not what it was for gay and lesbian-defined adolescents a decade ago: a confusion in their identities, which in the prior generation were so strongly under attack as manifestations of disease, illness, madness, criminality, signs and symptoms of nature gone astray, of sinful and antisocial appetites that threatened chaos to the social order. The youths we studied in Chicago at the Horizons agency came to have sufficient resources and role models that they could get beyond the story of confused identities and focus on the confusion that really troubled them: how to express their desires and identities in a homophobic society.

But even their experience is now dated. Today a new identity, being bisexual, is emerging to define relations with both genders. The concept of "bisexual" has been an important sense of identity since the last century, and most recently bisexuality and queer movements have become more popular in the United States, Canada, and, to a lesser extent, England and western Europe. Jay Paul and colleagues (1995, 377) have suggested that a sea change has occurred in relations between gays and bisexuals:

> This recognition of bisexuals by both the general public and the gay community as a distinct category (although they might be denigrated as either sexual anarchists or diseased pariahs) coincided with the development of a more organized bisexual movement protesting the forced invisibility and the stereotyping of bisexuals both in society at large and in the gay community. The growing acceptance of this life-style and label within the gay community is evidenced by the number of organizations that have shifted to the more inclusive term "lesbian, gay, and bisexual."

Bisexuality is more relevant to an understanding of sexual risk today and is probably more complicated than it was in the time of our original study. Many youths report that bisexuality is more acceptable and even approved than before. The emergence of queer nation and queer theory in activist and educated circles has certainly contributed to the impression that bisexuality is "cool." However, in just the same manner that socialization for AIDS sexual risk is enhanced through social institutions such as Horizons, and the absence of such leads to less education and prevention, we must raise a concern about the effect of bisexuality as a sexual identity in the current coming of age population. In general, there are far fewer "bisexual groups" that would step in to offer the sort of positive safer-sex education provided by gay and lesbian organizations or, in some instances, by public schools and clinics. The example of the bisexual center studied by Martin Weinberg and colleagues (1993) in San Francisco is instructive since AIDS education seemed less present in the cultural atmosphere and the center closed soon after their study was completed.

A more fully developed and socially acknowledged gay or lesbian identity in some contexts tends to reduce the risk of AIDS/HIV infection, both at the level of subjective perception of risk and at the level of objective behavior, because the person has available more knowledge and resources to make wise sexual decisions. In general, the overall effect of coming out in western settings brings greater involvement and identification with the gay and lesbian culture at the time, thereby reducing risk through greater self-protection. This trend is not completely surprising since a cross-country study that included Holland, the United States, England, and others more than twenty years ago demonstrated that positive mental health among gays and lesbians was associated with active involvement with the gay community (Williams and Weinberg 1974). Recently researchers in Holland found that when a gay man is comfortable with his sexuality and sexual lifeway (such as enjoying anal sex), he will then be more capable of taking the necessary steps to protect himself (De-Witt et al. 1994). In short, as gay sexual culture is consolidated, people can integrate their health into their social world.

One of the lessons from recent work on HIV risk and adolescent empowerment for sex education is instructive for rethinking the policy about antigay violence. Research shows consistently that simple knowledge of AIDS is not enough to instill safer sex or self-protection from the risk of HIV infection; other factors, such as poverty, power, resources, personal commitment, empowerment, and agency, are involved. At issue are empowerment and positive conviction in everyday life. The cultural "outness" of a person is a critical factor in his or her being able to negotiate vulnerability on the streets, in the classroom, and in the context of sexual encounters. Youths who are more secure in their identities in general are more immune to sexual risk-taking and reckless behavior. Being gay- or lesbian-identified and being out are certainly potential risks for the teenager. However, the economic disfranchisement of youths exacerbates the problems, where the disadvantaged and underprivileged teen may be exposed to multiple risks—poverty, physical violence, drug-taking, pressure from street gangs and peer groups.

Particularly in cities wherein "high-visibility" safe-sex campaigns and AIDS education and prevention efforts have had official endorsement, such as in Norway or Belgium, the general population has a fairly high awareness of the threat of AIDS. Compared to a decade ago, furthermore, we can no longer think of sexual disease as a problem of a "sexual minority" on the social fringe of what is forbidden or illegal.

The Magic Number of Homosexuals

This book is a critique of naive social constructionism and biological essentialism. Although I have written the book to open up a significant debate on what constitutes the social consciousness and desires of the gay or lesbian self and its cultural settings, we cannot ignore theories of essentialism and constructionism because these have shaped the questions asked and the perspectives taken in writing for at least a century. More recently, many gay and lesbian scholars and the public have wondered what contributions biology makes to desire and social roles. But it is the social constructionist, it seems to me, who must be addressed more fully now, simply because of the historical scholarship in the area. The idea came to me in concluding the study of gay and lesbian teenagers and their social rituals of coming out in Chicago. I pointed out the inherent paradox of gays and lesbians who refuse to take a stand on the issues of directly socializing those youths who desire the same sex. It is useful to reconsider the statistics and magical number of 10 percent in thinking about socializing youth.

Is it not the case that sexual identities are distributed differently across the United States? As we know, the recent Edward Laumann and colleagues (1994) national probability study of American sexuality found an average of adult homosexuality of only 2.5 percent for males and less for females. As the investigators have conceded, this rate is probably conservative and may be on the low side by 2 percent or so. I am interested in the impact of geographic locale and residence on the expression of same-gender sexual behavior. Clearly, as Kinsey (1948) noted in his study nearly a half century ago, the influence of the city and urban environment enhances the incidence of homosexual behavior.

But what we know from the most recent study today is just how significant this urban influence is. In the Laumann survey, a probability sample of urban cores in the United States found that men residing in large cities who were highly educated and white were the most likely to report sex with men. In the urban sample, one-third reported sex with women. Moreover, minority men were even more likely to report sex with men and women. Now when we factor in the data from the twelve largest cities in the United States, the effect of urban life is magnified. A 1995 article in the *Journal of Sex Research* on prevalence in the large survey studies in the United States (Binson et al. 1995) reveals that the incidence of men who report having same-sex partners in the general population rises from 2.6 to 7.8 percent. The incidence of men who report having same-sex partners in the next largest eighty-eight cities falls to 4.6 percent of the total population. The closer we come to the present, the higher the frequency becomes. Thus, from 1991 to 1995 aggregated data from the top twelve cities shows a rise to 11 percent from the 7.8 percent figure of all men who have same-gender partners. Finally, when we add in younger males, from age eighteen and up, the figure rises to its highest level of all—14.5 percent. To give an idea of the extremes of the spread of the prevalence of male homosexuality in the national probability sample, the incidence reported for the so-called rural counties sample (the chicken farmers of Arkansas) is very low—in the total aggregated sample of all males over age eighteen in rural counties the incidence falls to 2 percent of men who report having same-sex partners. In short, the incidence of gay men leading gay lives with partners is seven times higher in the biggest American cities than in rural counties. The magic number of 10 percent of all Americans being homosexual thus takes on a new meaning.

This is bad news for a simplistic and reductionistic biological theory of homosexuality that would predict, all things being equal, that we should find an invariant incidence of same-gender relationships among men in all times and places. Such a nonsensical theory grossly misstates the position, of course, since virtually all of the biopsychosocial theories of homosexuality explicitly or implicitly suggest that context and behavioral conditions may alter the phenotypic expression of the presumed universal genotypic traits (hormones, genes, etc.).

But the national incidence is good news for an understanding of the cultural and developmental interaction among the context of development, cultural attitudes regarding sexuality, and sexual behavior outcomes. Clearly, there is a social geography of desires and sexual lifeways in the United States. We can posit that rural versus urban contexts mediate the relationship between desires/preferences and sexual relationships. Homophobia can be conceptualized as a proxy for many of these mediators, although the construct of homophobia addresses the problem of individual differences in how a person grows up sexually and enters into sexual relations. The construct does not address the equally powerful problem of what the culture has to say about the expression of sexual variations. As time goes on we can expect to see a change that evens out the differences in rural and urban scenes, creating a more general sense of the formation of a gay and lesbian culture. This will not be the same in the United States and other western countries. But it will enhance the sense of a general social role and lifeway that may become more widely accepted at home and abroad.

◀ **7** ▶

Conclusion: Culture and Empowerment of Sexual Minorities

ACROSS THE WORLD THERE are peoples and cultures that acknowledge and accept the existence of same-gender desire among their own kind. They have not made this desire or sexual orientation into such an alien form that it had to be called an Other. Of course, their tolerance may be mixed with joking and teasing and mild stigma or sometimes with something worse. They may demand that everyone marry and produce children, and most people will comply with such an absolute demand; yet they may just as well tolerate forays into other relationships with the same gender. The range of examples offered in this book, although only a very small sample of the total, is still enough for us to understand how same-sex relations can be lived out in a cultural context of much greater tolerance, even happiness, in such places. Being considered a positive and definite part of human nature is an advantage for any human being. But a culture that regards homosexuality as a form of Otherness too alien to live near or love—as a sin, a disease, or a crime, as an immoral or antisocial act—makes life much harder not only to live but also to survive for those named as Other.

Many different lifeways have been noted in this book, but only those in the West are what we would regard as "gay or lesbian" today. As liberation movements and attempts to ameliorate the status of lesbians and gay men change, we become aware that there is no simple linear movement, forward into progress, at all times and places. Life does not hold out such a simple formula. Social and political democracy and acceptance of basic human rights of the individual are more commonly a backward and forward process—forward two steps and then back a step, back three steps and forward again around the corner. But in the course of recognizing this complicated politics, we can also seek to recognize and support the empowerment of people who desire the same gender. This is the simple point on which I want to close this study.

Sexuality is always part of a whole set of changes in the social and political economy, in the enlargement of gender relations, and in the avenues of expression for those who have same-gender desires. Tourism by western gays and lesbians is also a factor in the change. That the world system is growing to encompass everyone, however, must not confuse us into thinking that everyone is becoming "like us" or that westernization is an inevitable process that will erase all cultural differences, including sexual difference. Far from it; the lesson of anthropology suggests that cultures are vital and that they covet with pride their own traditions. Nevertheless, as change occurs and communication speeds up, the borrowing and altering of lifeways blend old and new, and this blending is a source of wonder.

Perhaps we should reiterate the importance of clarifying the difference between western and nonwestern lifeways. We should take care to avoid the tendency to "read" our own values and concepts into those of other cultures, the problems of ethnocentrism and sexual chauvinism raised in the beginning of this book. We should not look for a single model of gay and lesbian identities around the world any more than we should seek uniformity in how homosexuality was organized in the past. Rather, we should expect to find a plurality of homosexualities, with distinctive roles and beliefs, often with a long cultural history that cannot easily be displaced. The traveler from one culture to another is destined to encounter people and concepts that look like those back home. Such an intuition may be correct— or it may be false. The point is not to assume that the forms are the same, only that we can understand them with care and thought, if not some research. Cultures vary enormously in how they approve or disapprove of sexual behavior, as we have found, particularly when it comes to the acceptance or rejection of same-gender sexual relations. Likewise, significant differences across groups occur in how they approve or disapprove of sexuality outside of the context of marriage and reproduction; indeed, America has seen change within its own ideology, from an emphasis on reproduction to a focus on pleasure, particularly in the most recent sexual revolution of this century, which witnessed the rise of the lesbian and gay movement.

The traditional forms of same-gender homoerotic relations examined in these pages are distinctive totalities, sexual cultures, which embody lifeways. For these encompass the history, culture, persons, bodies, and minds of real people in real places who, in living life in those places, by necessity have had to accommodate their desires and their feelings about their bodies and sexuality into the local cultural traditions offered to them as they grew up. As the great classicist Kenneth Dover (1978, 203) once wrote on the ancient Greeks: "Homosexual relationships are not exhaustively divisible, in Greek society or in any other, into those which perform an educational function and those which provoke and relieve genital tension. Most relationships of any kind are complex, and the need for bodily contact and orgasm was one ingredient of the complex of needs met by homosexual eros."

Desire and accommodation to a culture form part of a larger system, the sum total of a sexual lifeway, neither fully chosen nor fully dictated. From one view, accommodation is domination; from another, acceptance, inclusion, and the feeling of belonging. These people who desired others of the same gender had no other way to fit into their communities and roles. We must not romanticize the two spirit and other traditional forms observed in this book. Their worlds were not perfect; indeed, it is lovely to read about and even think like them, but it would be a far lesser thing to have lived inside their skins and to have participated in their cultural realities. Neither is the cultural reality of contemporary society perfect; but I would choose it over any of the accounts of preliterate and nonwestern peoples we have studied in this book.

However, we must take care to avoid sexual chauvinism, too: We should not substitute our sexual reality, identity terms, or notions of beauty and gender and sexual desire for those of other people. Their cultural realities are constitutive of different forms of homosexuality than those objectified by the western tradition. The numerous accounts of anthropologists reviewed in this book, many of them wonderful gifts to the student of sexual nature and sexual culture, reflect the subjectification of the sexual in our own society as much as they point toward the emerging nations and globalization of sex. Through these rich and varied cultures, we begin to realize the hope of a true comparative study beyond anything bequeathed to us by Freud and the Victorian sexologists or the early anthropology of sexuality that discovered new lands.

In western culture over the centuries, desire for the same gender represented all that was evil and unnatural and could not be accepted into a conception of human nature that hated homoerotic relations. Love and romance, intimacy, and lifelong vows of commitment and partnership could never be part of homosexuality, it was mistakenly believed. Now a generation of people in many countries, making their lives together as partners in life, have proved this bias to be wrong. This false conception of homosexuality in the past reduced the whole person and his or her goals and aspirations to nothing more than sex, denying all of the full and loving person as well as his or her creativity, civility, and spirituality. We saw the damage that this did to non-Indian understandings of the two-spirit person among American Indians. The spirit and full personality were totally erased in the negative non-Indian conceptions of same-gender relations. Homophobia and discrimination were the product of this reductionism. Unfortunately, as we have also seen, the same western values were far too often exported to other cultures and imposed on them like a colonial regime imposes tax levies on a captive people. We see now that all such violations of the sexual lifeways of other peoples are not simply about sexuality; they are efforts to subjugate and justify the superior politics and religion of the colonizing culture.

The social construction of reality in same-gender relations throughout history and culture constantly reminds us of "us" and "them" stereotypes. They were recipes for exploitation. In many times and places the homosexual was identified as the Other or with Otherness and in the West as a monster or a disease. Same-gender relationships in nonwestern societies somehow interrupted the western cultural reality of sexuality and gender in a disturbing way. They challenged the dualisms of sex and gender. Such definitions of social reality and human nature—the idea of homosexuality in the cultural imagination of a people—are forever linked to social and cultural traditions in societies from ancient to modern times. Contrary to the western idea of homosexuality as secular or profane, even the antithesis of the sacred in the Judeo-Christian tradition, it has often been accepted and even admired in some other societies. Same-gender desire will have become better integrated into the western tradition when the morality of such desire is neither challenged nor treated as a special case but is instead understood to be a special kind of social and ontological form outside of these religious traditions; same-gender desire does not seek to erase them.

When the reductionistic and negative images of homosexuality in western cultures were exported to other places, along with the power and the means to punish native peoples, much violence was done against their sexual lifeways. This was wrong. What is remarkable is that such a distorted image went against the facts; in the cultures of Africa and New Guinea and Asia, same-gender relations were permitted or required in order to make their societies "work." For instance, we saw that in ancient Greece same-gender relations between older and younger males aimed to cultivate a certain spirit and being, a certain honor and manhood, a certain philosophical outlook that promoted free thought, all necessary in the creation of the Greek city and citizenship as lived in the ideals of age-graded homosexuality. Likewise, in New Guinea and elsewhere we have seen how same-gender relations were but a part of the larger pattern of social life, beginning in ceremonies in late childhood but fanning out over many years to include other areas of life: warrior training, religious and social exchanges, and the activities that involve a boy in marrying and having children. The desire for the same gender was part and parcel of the whole life and could not be reduced to less in such a life plan.

In American society the vulgar expression of sexual chauvinism and sexual moralism depicts heterosexuals as all "good" and homosexuals as all "bad," angels and devils. "The American passion for categorizing," Gore Vidal (1983, 211) once joked, "has now managed to create two nonexistent categories—gay and straight. Either you are one or the other. . . . You have to be one or the other." The charge of being "bad" is infectious; "although . . . therapists . . . and writers usually agree that those who desire the same-sex are not exactly criminals (in most of our states and in most circumstances they still are) or sinful . . . they must be, somehow, evil or inadequate or dangerous" (Vidal 1983, 211). The "naturalness" of the dichotomy heterosexual/homosexual has increasingly come under scrutiny but is always defended by authoritarian elements in society. As historian Jeffrey Weeks (1985, 204) has written, "The New Right throughout the West has targeted lesbian and gay movements and communities as sources of moral pollution and a measure of social decline."

Throughout the world a social and sometimes physical movement can be found among people who seek freedom and the ability to express their sexuality and desires. People will move from their village or hometown, out of the neighborhood, to another state or even another country, or go to another country as a tourist, in order to find a more tolerant attitude that accepts loving the same gender. In other cultures we have seen that sexual lifeways do not always look like those of the identities "gay" and "lesbian" as these are defined in the United States and similar western nations. It is true that the West is associated with the creation of distinctive sexual "communities" as a place to live and find a satisfying social life with others who love and desire the same gender. As we have seen in prior chapters, however, nonwestern cultures in many ways have tended to be more tolerant and accepting of these relationships than the complex societies of western civilization since the modern period introduced the strong dualism of homosexual/heterosexual.

Many other ideas can be traced as well to the emergence of sexual reform movements in Europe and North America since the late nineteenth century. Nonwestern sexual lifeways are no better or worse than those of other peoples—including ourselves. Granted, these elements may be present in the emergence of sexual minority communities, as we have seen in Africa, Mexico, Brazil, and Thailand. But we must guard against the expectation that merely by importing the western idea of "the autonomous individual" or the "gay role" and related Euro-American concepts, we will "solve" all the problems of those who desire the same gender in other cultures or even that they would accept this "solution." This is not the only way to empower people in helping them to lead the lives they choose.

It is a good thing to create more humane and positive laws for the protection of sexual minorities that desire the same gender, but more than that is needed. At issue is their social and psychological empowerment in the broader sense. Empowerment means being able to express and articulate desires and to build a rich and meaningful life that will use one's full productive potential. Empowerment also means being able to live a decent life with housing and food for the basic enjoyment of life. We have studied the process of coming out and compared this to coming of age ceremonies and found some parallels. Among gay and lesbian youths in the United States, their psychological and cultural "outness" is a decisive factor in their ability to protect themselves, to gain knowledge and a network of others who are helpful in the negotiation of homophobia, violence on the streets, everyday life in the classroom, and risk-taking in the context of sexual encounters. Withholding these resources is a danger and a liability to the psychological and social development of people. Youths who are more secure in their identities are less vulnerable to risk-taking and recklessness that would lead to HIV infection. When coupled with the absence of a community of others or a network of friends, the vulnerability that comes from hiding and the emotional and social inconsistency that results make the person more likely to take needless risks and in desperation to risk his or her life.

I opened this book with a tribute to Ruth Benedict, the great American anthropologist whose work from two generations ago continues to provide insights into how cultures create meaning in people's lifeways. Benedict (1938) cautions us to understand not only what people learn from culture but also what they must unlearn in order to adapt and be successful adults. She shows, for instance, that aggression may be completely permitted in childhood but forbidden among adults or that, in western nations such as the

United States, children are expected to be sexually naive but once they reach maturity, are expected to be sexually sophisticated even though they have received no training for such a role.

Her idea extends to same-gender desires and relations as well. Many people growing up in more tolerant environments may have experienced childhood sexual play with the same gender but subsequently had this tabooed or stopped, perhaps punished. Years later they may have come to understand that these desires never really went away; the culture communicated that they should be unlearned, but all that happened was that the feelings were repressed or the actions suppressed. Such conditions make for unsatisfying and unfulfilled lives, lives of quiet desperation, as Henry David Thoreau might have remarked.

The social change of the past two decades and the liberation of sexuality through reform movements like those of the gay and lesbian community in the United States have given a new and vital start to acceptance of same-gender relations in our country. It will take a few years more, perhaps another generation, but ultimately these desires will become accepted as part of the human nature of some individuals and therefore as part of the culture. Being gay or lesbian in our culture is thus an expression of a certain kind of desire and longing that may not be universal but is well enough known from culture and history to merit acceptance as an uncommon but general and divergent form of human nature in our species. The twenty-first century will indeed be here before we expect it, and with it will come a keener appreciation of gays and lesbians in all cultures; of this we can be sure.

◀ **Glossary** ▶

Bisexual—someone who engages in sexual behavior with both genders, though not necessarily at the same time or in the same way.

Erotic—anything that stimulates sexual arousal.

Gay—in the United States and most western countries, a man who erotically prefers the same gender, self-identifies as gay, and lives as openly gay.

Gay/lesbian—being a socially identified gay or lesbian person.

Gender—the culturally constituted organization of masculinity, femininity, and androgyny into culture categories and social roles.

Gender identity—the sense of feeling masculine, feminine, or androgynous.

Gender role—the social designation of conventional assignments of social status by gender, i.e., man, woman, boy, girl, mother, husband.

Heteroerotic—attraction and desire for the other gender.

Heteronormal—the postmodern idea that sexual lifeways and social existence are based on the norm of heterosexuality, specifically stipulating the need to marry and have children to be normal as the ultimate concerns in society.

Heterosexual—a normative moral category of personhood and sexual identity that stipulates exclusive lifelong sexual desire and erotic relations with the opposite gender.

Homoerotic—attraction and desire for the same gender.

Homophobia—the culturally constituted fear and hatred of homosexual persons, acts, events.

Homosexual—a normative moral category of personhood and sexual identity that stipulates exclusive, often clandestine sexual desire and erotic relations with the same gender.

Lesbian—a woman who prefers the same gender, self-identifies as a lesbian, and lives openly as lesbian.

Queer—the explicit identity queer, which resists being placed in any other category of social identity.

Queer theory—a deconstructive theory/movement that imagines alternatives to social reality, opposes normativity, and favors marginality, especially in treating heterosexualism as performativity and heteronormativity.

Sex—the biological differentiation of humans via genes, gonads, hormones, anatomy, etc. resulting in the classification male, female, and hermaphroditic.

Sexual culture—a historically conventionalized and shared system of sexual lifeways, supported by beliefs and gender/sexual roles and bounded as whole.

Sexual identity—the expression of sexual orientation in culturally constituted categories, such as homosexual/heterosexual.

Sexual lifeways—the culturally constituted worldview and sexual practices that are conventional or characteristic of a sexual culture.

Sexual orientation—the habitual preference for sexual desires, genders, and practices experienced as part of one's nature or being.

Sexuality—the total combination of biological sex and gender and erotic desires.

Third gender—anatomically normal male or female individuals whose culture assigns them to a conventional category of social being and action that is neither masculine nor feminine but is defined instead by a cultural classification such as "manly woman" or "two spirit."

Third sex—humans who are anatomically or behaviorally neither clearly male nor clearly female but hermaphroditic; this may be culturally organized into a separate category of sex assignment that leads to a distinctive gender and sexual identity.

◀ References ▶

Adam, Barry. 1986. "Age-Structured Homosexual Organization." In *Anthropology and Homosexual Behavior,* ed. E. Blackwood, pp. 1–34. New York: Haworth Press.

Bem, Daryl. 1996. "Exotic Becomes Erotic: A Developmental Theory of Sexual Orientation." *Psychological Review* 103:320–335.

Benedict, Ruth. 1934. *Patterns of Culture.* Boston: Houghton Mifflin.

_____. 1938. "Continuities and discontinuities in cultural conditioning." *Psychiatry* 1:161–167.

Besnier, Niko. 1994. "Polynesian Gender Liminality Through Time and Space." In *Third Sex, Third Gender: Beyond Sexual Dimorphism in Culture and History,* ed. G. Herdt, pp. 285–328. New York: Zone Books.

Binson, Diane, et al. 1995. "Prevalence and Social Distribution of Men Who Have Sex with Men: United States and Its Urban Centers." *Journal of Sex Research* 32, 3:245–254.

Blackwood, Evelyn. 1986. *The Many Faces of Homosexuality.* New York: Haworth Press.

Boswell, John. 1980. *Christianity, Social Tolerance, and Homosexuality.* Chicago: University of Chicago Press.

Boxer, Andrew, Judith A. Cook, and Gilbert Herdt. 1991. "To Tell or Not to Tell: Patterns of Self-Disclosure to Mothers and Fathers Reported by Gay and Lesbian Youth." In *Parent-Child Relations Across the Lifespan,* ed. K. Pillemer and K. McCartney, pp. 59–93. Oxford: Oxford University Press.

Butler, Judith. 1993. *Bodies That Matter: On the Discursive Limits of Sex.* New York: Routledge.

Carrier, Joseph. 1980. "Homosexual Behavior in Cross-Cultural Perspective." In *Homosexual Behavior: A Modern Reappraisal,* ed. J. Marmor, pp. 100–122. New York: Basic Books.

_____. 1995. *De los Otros: Intimacy and Homosexuality Among Mexican Men.* New York: Columbia University Press.

Chauncey, George Jr. 1994. *Gay New York*. New York: Basic Books.

Chodorow, Nancy J. 1992. "Heterosexuality as a Compromise Formation: Reflections on the Psychoanalytic Theory of Sexual Development." *Psychoanalysis and Contemporary Thought* 15:267–304.

D'Anglure, Bernardin Saladin. 1986. "Du foetus au chamane: La construction d'un 'troisieme sexe' Inuit." *Etudes Inuite* 10:25–113.

Deacon, A. B. 1934. *Malekula: A Vanishing People in the New Hebrides*. London: George Routledge.

D'Emilio, John. 1983. *Sexual Identities, Sexual Communities*. Chicago: University of Chicago Press.

D'Emilio, John D., and Estelle B. Freedman. 1988. *Intimate Matters: A History of Sexuality in America*. New York: Harper and Row.

Dekker, Rudolf M., and Lotte C. van de Pol. 1989. *The Tradition of Female Transvestitism in Early Modern Europe*. London: Macmillan.

Devereux, George. 1937. "Institutionalized Homosexuality Among the Mohave Indians." *Human Biology* 9:498–527.

DeWitt, John et al. 1994. "Behavioral Risk Reaction Strategies to Prevent HIV Infection Among Homosexual Men: A Grounded Theory Approach." *AIDS Education and Prevention* 6:493–505.

Dover, Kenneth J. 1978. *Greek Homosexuality*. Cambridge, Mass.: Harvard University Press.

Duberman, Martin et al. 1989. *Hidden from History: Reclaiming the Gay and Lesbian Past*. New York: NAL Books.

Dunton, Chris. 1989. "'Whyething Be That?' The Treatment of Homosexuality in African Literature." *Research in African Literature* 20:422–448.

Eliade, Mircea. 1951. *Shamanism*. New York: Basic Books.

Evans-Pritchard, E. E. 1970 "Sexual Inversion Among the Azande." *American Anthropologist* 72:1428–1434.

Fine, Michelle. 1988. "Sexuality, Schooling, and Adolescent Females: The Missing Discourse on Desire." *Harvard Education Review* 58:29–53.

_____. 1992. *Disruptive Voices: The Possibilities of Feminist Research*. Ann Arbor: University of Michigan Press.

Ford, Clelland S., and Frank A. Beach. 1951. *Patterns of Sexual Behavior*. New York: Harper and Brothers.

Foucault, Michel. 1980. *The History of Sexuality*. Trans. R. Hurley. New York: Viking.

Freud, Sigmund. [1905] 1962. *Three Essays on the Theory of Sexuality*. Reprint. New York: Basic Books.

Gagnon, John H. 1990. "The Explicit and Implicit Use of the Scripting Perspective in Sex Research." *Annual Review of Sex Research* 1:1–44.

Gay, Judith. 1986. "'Mummies and Babies' and Friends and Lovers in Lesotho." In *The Many Faces of Homosexuality: Anthropological Approaches to Homosexual Behavior,* ed. E. Blackwood, pp. 97–116. New York: Harrington Park Press.

Gevisser, Mark, and Edwin Cameron, eds. 1995. *Defiant Desire: Gay and Lesbian Lives in South Africa.* New York: Routledge.

Gillison, Gillian. 1993. *Between Culture and Fantasy: A New Guinea Highlands Mythology.* Chicago: University of Chicago Press.

Godelier, Maurice. 1986. *The Making of Great Men.* Cambridge: Cambridge University Press.

Greenberg, David. 1988. *The Construction of Homosexuality.* Chicago: University of Chicago Press.

Gregerson, Edgar. 1994. *The World of Human Sexuality.* New York: Irvington.

Gremaux, René. 1994. "Woman Becomes Man in the Balkans." In *Third Sex, Third Gender: Beyond Sexual Dimorphism in Culture and History,* ed. G. Herdt, pp. 241–285. New York: Zone Books.

Haldeman, Douglas C. 1994. "The Practice and Ethics of Sexual Orientation Conversion Therapy." *Journal of Consulting and Clinical Psychology* 62:221–227.

Halperin, David. 1990. *One Hundred Years of Homosexuality.* New York: Routledge.

Hart, C.W.M. 1963. "Contrasts Between Prepubertal and Postpubertal Education" In *Education and Culture,* ed. G. Spindler, pp. 400–425. New York: Holt, Rinehart and Winston.

Hekma, Gert. 1994. "A Female Soul in a Male Body: Sexual Inversion as Gender Inversion in Nineteenth-Century Sexology." In *Third Sex, Third Gender: Beyond Sexual Dimorphism in Culture and History,* ed. G. Herdt, pp. 213–240. New York: Zone Books.

Hendriksson, Benny, and Sven Axel Mansson. 1995. "Sexual Negotiations: An Ethnographic Study of Men Who Have Sex with Men." In *Culture and Sexual Risk,* ed. H. Brummelhuis and G. Herdt, pp. 157–182. New York: Gordon and Breach.

Herdt, Gilbert. 1981. *Guardians of the Flutes: Idioms of Masculinity.* New York: McGraw-Hill.

_____. 1982. "Fetish and Fantasy in Sambia Initiation." In *Rituals of Manhood,* ed. G. Herdt., pp. 44–98. Berkeley and Los Angeles: University of California Press.

_____. 1984a. "Ritualized Homosexuality in the Male Cults of Melanesia, 1862–1982: An Introduction." In *Ritualized Homosexuality in Melane-*

sia, ed. G. Herdt, pp. 1–81. Berkeley and Los Angeles: University of California Press.

_____. 1984b. "Semen Transactions in Sambia Culture." In *Ritualized Homosexuality in Melanesia,* ed. G. Herdt, pp. 167–210. Berkeley and Los Angeles: University of California Press.

_____. 1987a. "Homosexuality." In *The Encyclopedia of Religion,* 6:445–452. New York: Macmillan.

_____. 1987b. *The Sambia: Ritual and Gender in New Guinea.* New York: Holt, Rinehart and Winston.

_____. 1990. "Developmental Continuity as a Dimension of Sexual Orientation Across Cultures." In *Homosexuality and Heterosexuality: The Kinsey Scale and Current Research,* ed. D. Mcwhirter, J. Reinisch, and S. Sanders, pp. 208–238. New York: Oxford University Press.

_____. 1991a. "Representations of Homosexuality in Traditional Societies: An Essay on Cultural Ontology and Historical Comparison, Part I." *Journal of the History of Sexuality* 1:481–504.

_____. 1991b. "Representations of Homosexuality in Traditional Societies: An Essay on Cultural Ontology and Historical Comparison, Part II." *Journal of the History of Sexuality* 2:603–632.

_____. 1992. "'Coming Out' as a Rite of Passage: A Chicago Study." In *Gay Culture in America,* ed. G. Herdt, pp. 29–67. Boston: Beacon Press.

_____. 1993. "Introduction." In *Ritualized Homosexuality in Melanesia,* ed. G. Herdt, pp. vii–xliv. Berkeley and Los Angeles: University of California Press.

_____. 1994. "Mistaken Sex: Culture, Biology, and the Third Sex in New Guinea." In *Third Sex, Third Gender: Beyond Sexual Dimorphism in Culture and History,* ed. G. Herdt, pp. 419–446. New York: Zone Books.

_____, ed. 1989. *Gay and Lesbian Youth.* New York: Harrington Park.

_____. 1992. *Gay Culture in America: Essays from the Field.* Boston: Beacon Press.

_____. 1994. *Third Sex, Third Gender: Beyond Sexual Dimorphism in Culture and History.* New York: Zone Books.

Herdt, Gilbert, and Andrew Boxer. 1995. "Toward a Theory of Bisexuality." In *Concerning Sexuality: Approaches to Sex Research in a Postmodern World,* ed. R. Parker and J. Gagnon, pp. 69–84. New York: Routledge.

_____. 1996. *Children of Horizons: How Gay and Lesbian Youth Are Forging a New Way Out of the Closet.* Boston: Beacon Press.

Herdt, Gilbert, and Shirley Lindenbaum, eds. 1992. *The Time of AIDS.* Newbury Park, Calif.: Sage.

Herdt, Gilbert, and Robert J. Stoller. 1990. *Intimate Communications: Erotics and the Study of Culture.* New York: Columbia University Press.

Herek, Gregory. 1993. "The Context of Antigay Violence: Notes on Cultural and Psychological Heterosexism." In *Psychological Perspectives on Lesbian and Gay Male Experiences,* ed. L. Garnets and D. C. Kimmel, pp. 89–108. New York: Columbia University Press.

Herek, Gregory et al., eds. 1996. *Out in Force: Sexual Orientation and the Military.* Chicago: University of Chicago Press.

Herrell, Richard. 1992. "The Symbolic Strategies of Chicago's Gay and Lesbian Pride Day Parade." In *Gay Culture in America,* ed. G. Herdt, pp. 225–252. Boston: Beacon Press.

Hinsch, Bret. 1990. *Passions of the Cut Sleeve: The Homosexual Tradition in China.* Berkeley and Los Angeles: University of California Press.

Isay, Richard. 1996. *Becoming Gay: The Journey to Self-Acceptance.* New York: Pantheon Books.

Jackson, Peter. 1995. *Male Homosexuality in Thailand: An Interpretation of Contemporary Thai Sources.* New York: Global Academic.

Kinsey, Alfred et al. 1948. *Sexual Behavior and the Human Male.* Philadelphia: Saunders.

Knauft, Bruce. 1993. *South Coast New Guinea Cultures.* Cambridge: Cambridge University Press.

Kon, Igor. 1995. *The Sexual Revolution in Russia.* New York: Free Press.

Kulick, Don, and Margaret Willson, eds. 1995. *Taboo: Sex, Identity, and Erotic Subjectivity in Anthropological Fieldwork.* London: Routledge.

Lancaster, Roger. 1995. "That We Should All Become Queer." In *Conceiving Sexuality,* ed. R. Parker and J. Gagnon, pp. 135–156. New York: Routledge.

Lang, Sabine. 1996. "Travelling Woman: Conducting a Fieldwork Project on Gender Variance and Homosexuality Among North American Indians." In *Out in the Field,* ed. E. Lewin and W. Leap, pp. 86–110. Urbana: University of Illinois Press.

Laqueur, Thomas. 1990. *Making Sex: Body and Gender from the Greeks to Freud.* Cambridge, Mass: Harvard University Press.

Laumann, Edward O. et al. 1994. *The Social Organization of Sexuality.* Chicago: University of Chicago Press.

Lauretis, Teresa de. 1993. Introduction. "Queer Theory: Lesbian and Gay Sexualities." *Differences* 3 (Special issue):iii–xviii.

Leap, William L. 1996. *Word's Out.* Minneapolis: University of Minnesota Press.

Leupp, Gary P. 1996. *Male Colors: The Construction of Homosexuality in Tokugawa Japan.* Berkeley and Los Angeles: University of California Press.

Levine, Martin, John Gagnon, and Peter Nardi, eds. 1997. *In Changing Times: Gay Men and Lesbians Encounter HIV/AIDS.* Chicago: University of Chicago Press.

Lévi-Strauss, Claude. 1964. *The Savage Mind.* Chicago: University of Chicago Press.

Levy, Robert I. 1973. *The Tahitians.* Chicago: University of Chicago Press.

Lewin, Ellen, and William Leap, eds. 1996. *Out in the Field.* Urbana: University of Illinois Press.

Lumsden, Ian. 1996. *Machos, Maricones, and Gays: Cuba and Homosexuality.* Philadelphia: Temple University Press.

Malinowski, Bronislaw. 1929. *The Sexual Life of Savages in North-western Melanesia.* New York: Harcourt, Brace and World.

Martin, Emily. 1987. *The Woman in the Body.* Boston: Beacon Press.

Mead, Margaret. 1935. *Sex and Temperament in Three Primitive Societies.* New York: Dutton.

_____. 1961. "Cultural Determinants of Sexual Behavior." In *Sex and Internal Secretions,* ed. W. C. Young, pp. 1433–1479. Baltimore: Williams and Wilkins.

_____, ed. 1959. *An Anthropologist at Work: Writings of Ruth Benedict.* New York: Atherton Press.

Michaels, Stuart. 1996. "The Prevalence of Homosexuality in the United States." In *The Textbook of Homosexuality and Mental Health,* ed. R. P. Sabaj and T. S. Stein, pp. 43–63. Washington, D.C.: American Psychiatric Press.

Moodie, T. Dunbar, and Vivienne Ndatshe. 1994. *Going for Gold: Men, Mines, and Migration.* Berkeley and Los Angeles: University of California Press.

Morris, Robert J. 1992. "Same-Sex Friendships in Hawaiian Lore: Constructing the Canon." In *Oceanic Homosexualities,* ed. S. O. Murray, pp. 71–102. New York: Garland.

Murphy, Timothy. 1992. "Redirecting Sexual Orientations: Techniques and Justifications." *Journal of Sex Research* 29:501–523.

Murray, Stephen O. 1992. "Male Homosexuality in Japan Before the Meiji Restoration." In *Oceanic Homosexualities,* ed. S. O. Murray, pp. 111–150. New York: Garland.

_____. 1996. *American Gay.* Chicago: University of Chicago Press.

Nanda, Serena. 1990. *Neither Man nor Woman.* Belmont, Calif.: Wadsworth.

National Study Team. 1994. *National Study of Sexual and Reproductive Knowledge and Behaviour in Papua New Guinea.* Goroka, Papua New Guinea: National Institute of Medical Research.

Newton, Esther. 1993. *Cherry Grove, Fire Island—Sixty Years in America's First Gay and Lesbian Town.* Boston: Beacon Press.

Parker, Richard. 1991. *Bodies, Pleasures, and Passions: Sexual Culture in Contemporary Brazil.* Boston: Beacon Press.

Patterson, Charlotte. 1995. "Lesbian Mothers, Gay Fathers, and Their Children." In *Lesbian, Gay, and Bisexual Identities over the Lifespan,* ed. A. R. D'Augelli and C. J. Patterson, pp. 262–291. New York: Oxford University Press.

Paul, Jay P. et al. 1995. "The Impact of the HIV Epidemic on the U.S. Gay Male Communities." In *Lesbian, Gay, and Bisexual Identities over the Lifespan,* ed. A. R. D'Augelli and C. J. Patterson, pp. 347–397. New York: Oxford University Press.

Pflugfelder, Gregory M. 1992. "Strange Fates: Sex, Gender, and Sexuality in Torikaebaya Monogatari." *Monumenta Nipponica* 47:347–368.

Plant, Richard. 1989. *The Pink Triangle: The Nazi War Against Homosexuals.* New York: Henry Holt.

Posner, Richard. 1992. *Sex and Reason.* Chicago: University of Chicago Press.

Prieur, Annick. 1994. "I Am My Own Special Creation: Mexican Homosexual Transvestites' Construction of Femininity." *Young: Nordic Journal of Youth Research* 2:3–17.

Read, Kenneth E. 1980. *Other Voices.* Novato, Calif.: Chandler and Sharp.

Rich, Adrienne. 1980. "Compulsive Heterosexuality and Lesbian Existence." *Signs* 5:631–660.

Ringrose, Kathryn M. 1994. "Living in the Shadows: Eunuchs and Gender in Byzantium." In *Third Sex, Third Gender: Beyond Sexual Dimorphism in Culture and History,* ed. G. Herdt, pp. 85–110. New York: Zone Books.

Robinson, Paul. 1976. *The Modernization of Sex: Havelock Ellis, Alfred Kinsey, William Masters, and Virginia Johnson.* Ithaca: Cornell University Press.

Rocke, Michael. 1988. Sodomites in Fifteenth-Century Tuscany. *Journal of Homosexuality* 16:17–31.

Roscoe, Will. 1991. *The Zuni Man-Woman.* Albuquerque: University of New Mexico Press.

_____. 1994. "How to Become a Berdache." In *Third Sex, Third Gender: Beyond Sexual Dimorphism in Culture and History*, ed. G. Herdt, pp. 329–372. New York: Zone Books.

Royce, Anya Peterson. 1987. "Masculinity and Femininity in Elaborated Movement Systems." In *Masculinity/Femininity: Basic Perspectives*, ed. J. M. Reinisch, pp. 315–343. New York: Oxford University Press.

Sankar, Andrea. 1986. "Sisters and Brothers, Lovers and Enemies: Marriage Resistance in Southern Kwangtung." In *Anthropology and Homosexual Behavior*, ed. E. Blackwood, pp. 69–82. New York: Haworth Press.

Sedgwick, Eve Kosofsky. 1990. *Epistemology of the Closet*. Berkeley and Los Angeles: University of California Press.

Smith, Bruce K. 1991. *Homosexual Desire in Shakespeare's England: A Cultural Poetics*. Chicago: University of Chicago Press.

Smith-Rosenberg, Carroll. 1985. *Disorderly Conduct: Visions of Gender in Victorian America*. New York: Knopf.

Stimpson, Catharine R. 1996. "Women's Studies and Its Discontents." *Dissent* 43:67–75.

Stoller, Robert J. 1979. *Sexual Excitement*. New York: Pantheon Books.

_____. 1985. *Observing the Erotic Imagination*. New Haven: Yale University Press.

Stoller, Robert J., and Gilbert Herdt. 1985. "Theories of Origins of Homosexuality: A Cross-Cultural Look." *Archives of General Psychiatry* 42:399–404.

Teunis, Niels F. 1996. "Homosexuality in Dakar: Is the Bed the Heart of a Sexual Subculture?" *Journal of Gay, Lesbian, and Bisexual Identity* l:153–170.

Trumbach, Randolph. 1994. "London's Sapphists: From Three Sexes to Four Genders in the Making of Modern Culture." In *Third Sex, Third Gender: Beyond Sexual Dimorphism in Culture and History*, ed. G. Herdt, pp. 111–136. New York: Zone Books.

Van Baal, Jan. 1966. Dema: *Description and Analysis of Marind-anim Culture*. The Hague: Martinus Nijhoff.

Van der Meer, Theo. 1994. "Sodomy and the Pursuit of a Third Sex in the Early Modern Period." In *Third Sex, Third Gender: Beyond Sexual Dimorphism in Culture and History*, ed. G. Herdt, pp. 137–212. New York: Zone Books.

Vance, Carole S. 1991. "Anthropology Rediscovers Sexuality: A Theoretical Comment." *Social Science and Medicine* 33:875–884.

Vidal, Gore. 1983. *Pink Triangle and Yellow Star*. London: Granada.

Weeks, Jeffrey. 1985. *Sexuality and Its Discontents*. London: Routledge and Kegan Paul.

Weinberg, Martin S. et al. 1993. *Dual Attraction: Understanding Bisexuality*. New York: Oxford University Press.

Westermark, Edward. 1917. *The Origin and Development of the Moral Ideas*. 2d ed. Vol. 2. London: Macmillan.

Weston, Kath. 1993. "Lesbian/Gay Studies in the House of Anthropology." *Annual Review of Anthropology* 22:339–367.

Williams, Martin S., and Colin W. Weinberg. 1974. *Male Homosexuals: Their Problems and Adaptations*. New York: Oxford University Press.

Williams, Walter. 1986. *The Spirit and the Flesh: Sexual Diversity in American Indian Culture*. Boston: Beacon Press.

Wilson, Carter. 1995. *Hidden in the Blood: A Personal Investigation of AIDS in the Yucatan*. New York: Columbia University Press.

Wolf, James, ed. 1989. *Gay Priests*. New York: HarperCollins.

Young-Bruehl, Elisabeth. 1996. *The Anatomy of Prejudices*. Cambridge, Mass.: Harvard University Press.

◀ About the Book ▶
and Author

THIS NEW AUTHORITATIVE STUDY of gays and lesbians presents a unique perspective on maturing and living within ancient and contemporary societies that provide a place for same-gender desires and relations.

Gilbert Herdt reveals patterns of same-gender relations that offer provocative new insights on change occurring in the emerging understanding of gay and lesbian lives. Accurate in both its scientific conceptions and its wealth of cultural and historical material, the book gives examples ranging from ancient Greece and feudal China and Japan to the developing countries of Africa, India, Mexico, Brazil, and Thailand; from a New Guinea society to contemporary U.S. culture, including Native Americans. For all of these peoples, homoerotic relations emerge as part of their culture, not apart from history or society. In many of these groups, loving or engaging in homosexual relations is found to be the very basis of the local cultural theory of "human nature" and the mythological basis for the cosmos and the creation of society.

The most important lesson to learn from this cross-cultural and historical study of homosexuality is that there is room for many at the table of humankind in societies around the world. Herdt contends that modern western culture is mistaken in continuing the legislation of prejudice against lesbians and gays. He shows us that gay and lesbian practice is treated as an acceptable, natural expression of human nature in most other cultures, from ancient to contemporary times. Ultimately, what emerges from Herdt's observations of love and sex in other cultures is a long-overdue documentation of homoerotic relations as part of the fabric of any culture, not as a separate, deviant lifestyle, as so many of us have been taught.

Gilbert Herdt is professor of human development and director of the Center for Culture and Mental Health at the University of Chicago. He is the author of numerous articles and fifteen books, including *Guardians of the Flutes: Idioms of Masculinity* and *Sambia: Ritual and Gender in New Guinea,* and he is coauthor of *Children of Horizons: How Gay and Lesbian Youth Are Forging a New Way Out of the Closet.* He resides in Chicago and Amsterdam.

◀ Index ▶